Ted & Lorraine Bloemhof
17851 Palm Ave
Shafter, CA 93263-9754

Jesus Christ at Face Value

Is He For Real?

Volume I

James L. Unger

A fictional account about people
who knew Him or knew about Him,
based on the Gospels of the Bible.

*To Pastor Stahn, a brother
in the ministry;*

Rev. J. L. Unger.

Treasure House

An Imprint of

Destiny Image

P.O. Box 310

Shippensburg, PA 17257

"For where your treasure is
there will your heart be also." Matthew 6:21

ISBN 1-56043-781-2

For Worldwide Distribution
Printed in the U.S.A.

Treasure House books are available through these fine distributors outside the United States:

Christian Growth, Inc.
Jalan Kilang-Timor, Singapore 0315

Successful Christian Living
Capetown, Rep. of South Africa

Lifestream
Nottingham, England

Vision Resources
Ponsonby, Auckland, New Zealand

Rhema Ministries Trading
Randburg, South Africa

WA Buchanan Company
Geebung, Queensland, Australia

Salvation Book Centre
Petaling, Jaya, Malaysia

Word Alive
Niverville, Manitoba, Canada

Contents

Foreword

One of the goals of every Christian pastor and teacher is to help those who are exposed to the Bible to experience that special "moment of truth." That is when the reality of Jesus Christ and all that He is, and all that He came to do in the lives of ordinary human beings, registers as part of God's unfolding redemptive plan for every one of us—providing we believe and respond.

James Unger has accomplished something very significant in helping ordinary people—which of course means the whole lot of us—to understand spiritual concepts. He does this through a series of accounts about people who became personally aware of the reality of Jesus Christ. These individuals were eyewitnesses to what God was unfolding in their presence through Jesus Christ.

It is a rare thing to find a lucid style of writing combined with careful and thorough biblical research. The embellishment of a creative imagination that draws upon inferences from the biblical record makes this work particularly unique. Once we begin with the author to imagine what must have been said and done in response to Jesus of Nazareth, our understanding is marvelously illuminated. Through Him, God invaded our world, both individually and in all of human society.

This book, and its companion volume, makes the people who encountered Jesus come to life for us. Through Him, they not only experienced God's power in this world, but became equipped for the next. Because of their encounters with Christ, the power of God entered the equation of their experience, and they were never to be the same again!

The Rev. Dr. Donald P. Buteyn
Senior Pastor
First Presbyterian Church
Bakersfield, California

Introduction

For centuries the Bible has been the world's most widely distributed book—more so now than ever before. Wherever there are Christians, there the Bible will be found. It tells it like it is; it shows us who God is; and it tells us what kind of persons He wants us to be.

There are thousands of people, however, who possess that Book of books, yet have never discovered that the individuals portrayed in its pages were indeed humans. True enough, they lived a different lifestyle than may be our experience in this last decade of the 20th Century, but their basic natures were like our own. These people worked and lived with what they had. So do we.

Suddenly, a man named Jesus of Nazareth burst upon the human scene. He declared with superhuman power that the God who created us was not a remote and disinterested Deity. He didn't attempt to prove God's existence philosophically or scientifically, but instead simply stated that God existed without question and proceeded to introduce this God-above-all-gods as our Heavenly Father. Jesus introduced Himself as God's only begotten Son (John 3:16). He showed us who God is and what we were intended to be like. The fact that Jesus was God in a person—a human being—could only be described to us through the analogy of the intimate relationship between a father and his son.

The pages that follow contain the stories of people who faced the crisis of a personal encounter with this Man from Nazareth. In these accounts, you will learn about the background and the personal characteristics of these people. They are not characters in a fictional story; these people were blood and bone, soul-possessing human beings. You will be present as the silent observer at their individual encounters with Christ. You will witness the crisis that develops for them from their encounters. And you will discover their responses to those experiences, and what happened to them as a result.

I have added some descriptive detail to these stories through the process of noting the influence of the customs of the times and places, and by creating appropriate dialogue and actions. I recommend that the reader keep a Bible handy to look up references which are not directly quoted, in order to achieve a more complete understanding of each person's encounter.

This book has been arranged so that it can be read by an individual or be used as a resource for Bible study discussion groups. It can also be used for dramatic presentations or other similar purposes. Each chapter can stand alone, though some of the information given in one chapter may overlap into another (the influence of John the Baptist, for example).

This work is the outgrowth of a series of Bible studies which I originally presented to an adult class in the spring of 1974 at the First Presbyterian Church of Seattle, Washington. The response of those who heard them at that time, plus the response of those who have heard them presented as sermons, convinced me that others would also find them to be encouraging and strengthening to their faith. My prayer is that the living Jesus Christ will bring about an encounter with many readers, who as a result will find a whole new purpose in living.

At the end of this volume you will find a section called "Real Discoveries," which is a series of questions designed to provoke thought and discussion. These will be helpful for youth or adult study groups. There are no right or wrong answers, except as they may lead to a new perspective in your life with Christ.

* * * * *

A second volume of other New Testament people under the same title will also be available for further reading and inspiration.

About the title to these volumes:

The "Face Value" of a life insurance policy is the amount it will pay in the event of death as stipulated within the policy. The credibility of the company issuing the policy determines whether you will actually receive what the policy promises.

The people described in this volume had to decide for themselves if Jesus Christ was all that He claimed to be. They had to accept Him at "face value." So do we!

Is He for real?

James L. Unger
1993

Chapter 1

Joseph: A Common Man

Joseph was more than a "common" man, but he didn't know it. Chosen to be the "appointed" father of the Son of God forced a crisis upon him that no other man in history has had to face.

If it is proper to call a man such as Joseph a "common" man, then we would do well to define what we mean by that word. If it is common for a man to settle down, support his family, learn and pursue a trade, pay his taxes, live with the respect of his neighbors, and be faithful to his religious convictions, then Joseph was a common man.

But Joseph's influence on the character and teachings of Jesus, his "supernatural Son," proves that there is no way he should be regarded as a "common" man. We can also find the characteristics of this humble man inbred into his natural son, James, the author of the New Testament book which bears his name. Much of Jesus' Sermon on the Mount parallels James' book. The Scriptures give us only a few brief descriptions of Joseph (Matthew 1, 2, and 13; Luke 1 and 2). Enough is said, however, to learn that Joseph had to make one of the most difficult decisions of any man we know about since Abraham reluctantly agreed to offer his son, Isaac, as a sacrifice to God (Genesis 22:1-19). Abraham and Joseph compare favorably as great men of faith.

Given the genealogical evidence we have of the varying names in the lists in Matthew, Chapter 1, and Luke, Chapter 3, we learn that Joseph was of royal lineage from the great King David of Israel. Though Jesus' family tree is traced back to this royal heritage, it was done through Joseph, not Mary, who was His only natural parent. This is why Joseph had to go to Bethlehem, the city of David, to be registered and to pay his government taxes.

Royalty in his blood line apparently gave Joseph no particular status in his home town of Nazareth. At that time, Nazareth was located on an east-west trade route about half way between Lake Galilee and the Mediterranean Sea. A Roman army post was located there which served as the headquarters for the garrison occupying that part of Galilee. The city was located on the northwest edge of the Valley of Esdraelon, near Magiddo (or Armageddon), where over centuries many battles had been fought with Israel's invaders.

Nazareth was not a very desirable "family" type of town. Its reputation was considered less than good. Nathaniel, who became one of Jesus' disciples about thirty years later, remarked just before being introduced to Jesus, "Nazareth! Can anything good come from there?" All of the vices usually associated with a military base could be found there.

Obviously, even though a resident of Nazareth may have been able to trace his heritage back to Israel's most heroic king, it wouldn't have been all that smart to flaunt that piece of information too loudly with a foreign occupation army on his very doorstep.

Despite the reputation of the town and the constant threat of the ruthless oppressors, Joseph managed to establish his home and make a reasonable livelihood as a carpenter. Undoubtedly he was very much in demand, since he was apparently able to support a large family through his occupation. He could hardly have worked around the town without doing some jobs as a stonemason, too, for most of the buildings were made of white limestone.

Though the Jews had a variety of reasons for hating their Roman oppressors, it seems that Joseph must have related to them as fellow human beings. And they must have regarded him in the same way. When the time came to be registered and taxed, there was little reluctance on his part to make the difficult and dangerous trip south to Bethlehem. Granted, he had little choice. But there is no scriptural reason to believe that he was a militant rebel.

Joseph was probably older than the lovely young lady to whom he was engaged, perhaps by several years. Some have even thought that he may have been a childless widower, whose intention was to marry a young woman by whom he could have a son. This was considered the highest achievement a Jewish man could attain. He demonstrated a genuine and deep love for her through his care and protection of her life. But aside from this fact, a young woman would have a better chance of bearing him a larger family, which indeed Mary eventually did.

First and foremost among the principles by which Joseph directed his life was that of morality, being described as "a righteous man" (Matthew 1:19). One's imagination does not have to stretch too far to visualize Joseph's shock and horror when he learned that Mary, to whom he was engaged, was pregnant.

This man's nature was normally calm, and he was able to take life pretty well as it came. But if there was ever a situation that would cause him to come "unglued" (to use a carpenter's term), this was certainly it. The local Jewish community—if they found out—would regard him as an overanxious man who had taken advantage of his young fiancée long before their wedding. Much more severely would they regard his bride-to-be, Mary! Both would be condemned for a moral sin! Though unwed pregnancies happen in every generation, it was especially serious among the Jewish social structures of that day.

But the unborn child wasn't Joseph's, and he knew it, for they had not yet come together. Whose was it then? Had Mary, who seemed so mature and devout, so morally dependable and decent, actually deceived him? Or had she been raped by one of those Romans from the army base? If such a thought crossed his mind, and it must have, his hatred for the Romans would have raged almost beyond control. Nothing could have been worse in those days than to bear a child resulting from rape—half Jewish and half Roman.

Even with this dark cloud of controversy hovering over them, Joseph and Mary proceeded with their wedding though Joseph could not complete their relationship until this mystery was solved.

Certainly, this baby was inconvenient. Joseph knew it was not *their* child. But taking its life by abortion was not even an option for this devout couple. Joseph must have thought to himself, *What should I do now?* For the sakes of Mary and the baby soon to be born, the options were few for this righteous man.

There was only one thing he could do: give Mary a quiet divorce, take her out of the community, and then provide support for her and the baby.

There was Zacharias, a priest who lived in the hills of Judea to the south and his wife, Elizabeth, who was Mary's cousin. Joseph knew Elizabeth would take good care of Mary, and the couple, being older in years, could be like a father and mother to Mary and the baby. That seemed to be the best solution.

Joseph was exhausted with the pressure of this dilemma, and his hopes for a family of his own, with Mary as his companion, were dashed. One night, he laid down on his bed as helpless and flat as were those precious dreams.

Mary had not told him of her secret rendezvous with the angel of God (Luke 1:26-38). No one would believe her, especially a practical, hard working man like Joseph. He wasn't given to believing in such visions or being so heavenly-minded. His feet were planted firmly on the earth.

As with many people who are in the midst of a severe crisis, Joseph had what must have started out to be a nightmare. An angel of God appeared to him. Joseph's initial response was absolute rebellion. He writhed about and uttered in his dream, "Why weren't you guarding Mary when this happened to her? What are you trying to do to us? Neither of us deserve this kind of treatment! How is it that you would allow this disgrace to fall upon us when all we wanted was to live a decent and peaceful life from the start?

"How could you allow some 'dog' from the army base to rape Mary and tear our lives apart? We haven't even had a chance to come together yet, and here she is already involved in what can only turn out to be a scandal that will follow her for the rest of her life! If she winds up to be a moral wreck, it's your fault, and you can tell that to God!"

Then amid his fatigue, confusion, anger and shredded spirit, the angel came closer. Extending a hand and speaking in a strangely comforting and quiet voice, the angel said, "Joseph, son of David, do not be afraid to take Mary home as your wife, because what is conceived in her is from the Holy Spirit. She will give birth to a Son, and you are to give Him the name Jesus, because He will save His people from their sins" (Matthew 1:20-21). With that, the angel vanished and the dream was over. Joseph slept the deep sleep of the spent man that he was.

The sun awakened him and he heard the usual sound of tramping feet as the soldiers marched nearby through the narrow streets of Nazareth. Drill sergeants barked out their calls, which echoed off the buildings and disrupted the quiet of the hill upon which the town was set. Nothing outside had changed.

The dream almost forgotten, Joseph sat at the breakfast table silently and in deep thought as Mary served him. Nothing had changed inside his house either. Mary was still pregnant, and the child was still not his.

Joseph got up from the table without saying a word and walked to the small synagogue nearby for his morning prayers. The rabbi (teacher) read from the holy scrolls the words of the Prophet Isaiah, "Therefore the Lord Himself will give you a sign: The virgin will be with child and will give birth to a son, and will call Him Immanuel" (Immanuel means "God with us") (Isaiah 7:10,14). Joseph only half listened to the first part of the reading.

As he sat there, the full impact of that passage began to sink in. Not only had he studied the prophets before with the men of the synagogue, but as he heard them this time, the dream of the previous night with the comforting words of that angel came upon him like a summer cloudburst.

Joseph abruptly stood up, again not saying a word, and ran home. He led Mary to a chair, and then sat down in another chair in front of her. He clamped his big calloused hands on her shoulders and demanded, "Mary, tell me what you know about this baby!"

With soft but puzzled eyes, Mary looked right into his and realized his firm determination. She spoke hesitatingly, "Joseph, if I tell you, you won't understand what I'm saying, because such a thing can't happen— yet it did!" Joseph persisted. She continued, "I had a

8

vision, yet it wasn't a vision exactly. An angel of the Lord came..." Joseph interrupted, "And he told you that you were going to bear a son, right?" His voice became more intense. "And he is to be the Saviour of Israel, right? And you are still a virgin, right?"

Mary's mouth fell open. She was completely stunned. "How did you know? I haven't told a soul because I was sure nobody would ever believe me!" Joseph, usually the calm, collected, mature business-man, threw his arms high in the air and leaped out of his chair shouting at the top of his bass voice, "Hallelujah! Hallelujah! Glory to God in the High-est!" Over and over he shouted his relief.

The soldiers, still drilling in the streets nearby couldn't keep their cadence. A cat tracking a mouse outside the house turned in fright and ran up a tree. A small child playing outside ran crying to his mother. The neighbors, having known that some-thing had been very wrong in Joseph's house lately, understood that now something was very right.

Soon Joseph, with big tears streaming down his rugged face, eventually got his feet back on the earth again. Mary was still in shock as he threw his mus-cular arms around her and squeezed her lightly. "Mary," he panted, "I want you to live with Elizabeth and Zacharias for a while so I can get things ready for the baby here. That way the neighbors won't gossip—at least not where you will hear it. Then you won't be a temptation to me either, for this son must be born as God ordered—to a virgin!"

A few months later, the house was ready for Mary and supplied with the baby furniture that Joseph had built. So Mary returned home. Then Joseph received the expected order from the government to go to Bethlehem to be registered and to pay his taxes. He led his donkey carrying Mary to the hill country where Zacharias and Elizabeth lived, and there saw the couple's new baby, born by another miracle. They were too old to have children, or so they had thought. Elizabeth had passed the change of life. Joseph was about to ask how this was possible when Mary put her finger over his lips and said, "Let's go and I'll tell you later" (see Luke 1:5-80).

The couple made their way to Bethlehem. But— the crowds! It appeared that David sure had a lot of descendants. No room in this hotel or that one. But a sympathetic "desk clerk" told them that because of Mary's condition, he would put together a bed in an animal stall if they wanted it. Joseph, aware of their plight, reluctantly sighed, "We'll take it."

In the stillness of the early morning just before dawn, it happened. Joseph, with a gentleness uncommon to his rough-skinned hands, delivered this most precious of babies and laid Him on top of Mary while he completed the delivery. The labor had not been as hard as might have been expected after such a long donkey ride. Mary wrapped the baby tightly in a blanket, for the morning was cool.

Just as the sun was making its way over the horizon, a few young men arrived at the stall. They seemed bewildered, yet they appeared to have found what they were looking for. Joseph, fearful at first because of their unkempt appearance, supposed that they might be hoodlums intent on robbery. With the crowds of people in Bethlehem, there undoubtedly were some undesirables among them.

The oldest of the men spoke in a barely audible whisper. "We shepherds had a strange thing happen to us up in the hills. A person who looked like an angel... " Joseph, chuckling to himself, looked at Mary and whispered, "That angel has sure been busy!" The shepherd went on, "...This angel came and said that we would find a newborn baby who was to be a Saviour known as Christ the Lord, lying in a manger. We knew that no one who lived in Bethlehem would be having a baby in a stable, so it had to be happening to someone from out of town. We inquired at the hotels, and here we are."

The shepherds quietly stepped forward to see what this child was like. One of the others spoke up, "After that angel told us this, a whole lot of them seemed to fill the sky, and they were shouting and singing something like, 'Glory to God in the

Highest'...." Those words of praise were not new to
Joseph and Mary.

+ + + + +

Many of us have found ourselves rebelling against
God in the face of upsetting, tragic, or frightening
circumstances. We know that such events come into
the lives of many people who are unprepared for
such calamity, and we understand how that could
happen to us as well. It's just that we don't like
being blamed for their happening, and we don't like
those we love to be blamed either. So isn't it "common" to thrash about in rebellion saying, "Why did
this happen to me?" This is the crisis that Joseph encountered and led to the event that changed his life—
and changed the world!

No amount of rebelling or outcry against circumstances, people or God Himself will give you the
answer you want. At times He allows us to exhaust
ourselves to the point where the rebellion wears
down and the openness and willingness to listen
begins. Then, in that quiet but firm inner voice, God
helps us put our lives together again.

Joseph's monumental calling in life was to support and raise the most influential Person who ever
lived, and his preparation for that duty wasn't easy.
Perhaps most of us are not destined for the good or
easy life either. Few people are. Wouldn't real prog-
ress be made if the rebellion ceased and God's work
could begin?

Chapter 2

Mary: A Mother With an Uncommon Son

God often calls His choicest servants out of circumstances and backgrounds that we would expect could produce only the opposite of what God would be looking for.

This may not prove or disprove any sociological principle concerning the influence of heredity or environment. However, because God calls whomever He will to do what He needs to have done, He prepares that person for his or her life's purpose in His own way. Sometimes the results He achieves in the person He acts upon are in direct contradiction to the heritage and/or environment from which that person came.

Matthew tells us nothing of the angel's announcement to Mary. Luke tells us very little about

Mary's background except that she was at Nazareth when the angel, Gabriel, came to meet her. She was at that time a young virgin and was engaged to a man named Joseph. We may assume that she either lived in Nazareth or was visiting from the hill country of Judea. That is where her cousin, Elizabeth, lived with her husband, Zacharias, the local priest. As to whether Mary was an orphan or was simply not close to her parents, even after she became pregnant, we can only speculate (Luke 1:26-45). All we can say for certain is that her parents are not mentioned.

We can assume by the profound depth and historical insight of the song she composed after the angel's announcement of Jesus' birth (Luke 1:46-55), that Mary had been well trained in the Jewish faith. This would lead us to think that she had been living near or with Elizabeth and Zacharias for some time and had been taught in their home. It was not common in those times for a Jewish girl to obtain her education outside of the home, particularly if she came from a poor family.

Whether she was from Nazareth or from the hill country of Judea, Mary was indeed quite different from a typical teenage girl. Her trust in God was deep and personal. Most girls were still in their teens when they became engaged. As was the common Jewish custom of the day, whoever was responsible for Mary's care probably arranged her engagement to Joseph. Having her married to a settled, hard working craftsman would have been a real source of pride and relief for her family, knowing that her proper care and welfare would be adequately provided by him.

Though a virgin, she was under no delusions as to the role of a man in conceiving a child. It would appear by Luke's description that even though she was troubled and puzzled about the angel's sudden appearance, she was not overwhelmingly frightened. The first thing she said in reply to the angel was, "How will this be, since I am a virgin?" (Luke 1:34). If the wording in other versions is correct, then the idea of having a child by any man other than by her husband was totally outside Mary's thoughts: "How can this be, since I have no husband?" Being trained in the strong moral standards of the Jewish faith, this would have been a natural response for her to give.

She was not frightened, at least not after Gabriel assured her with the words, "Do not be afraid, Mary, you have found favor with God" (Luke 1:30). Whereas the angel spoke later to Joseph through a dream, Mary's experience with Gabriel is described as a direct conversation face to face, in person. It seems that Mary was not easily rattled by sudden events, and this characteristic reappears several times throughout her life. Most certainly she was contemplative, but there was a steadiness that became an integral ingredient of her personality. This also suggests that she may have previously experienced some great trauma in her young life, such as the death of her parents. God prepared Mary well to be the mother of His Son.

The blessings of her distinct honor must have been reinforced by the strong hand of Joseph at her side as they made their way to Bethlehem to register and pay their taxes. He was also there as the most precious baby ever born was delivered in the animal stall. Even if their marriage had been arranged by her father or a guardian, their love is evident in the moving scene of Jesus' birth. Christians everywhere remember and celebrate this same love story every Christmas in the closest family activity of the year, as we reflect back to the manger scene.

Ominous clouds hung over this little family almost from the time of Jesus' birth. Eight days after His birth, Mary and Joseph took Jesus to the temple in Jerusalem to have Him circumcised and to fulfill the Jewish rite of Mary's purification ceremony.

There they met an old prophet of the temple named Simeon. He came over to them and, perhaps even surprisingly, took the Child in his arms. He offered a beautiful blessing and then prophesied what would almost seem to be a curse upon Mary. In grave tones he spoke, "This Child is destined to cause the falling and rising of many in Israel, and to be a sign that will be spoken against, so that the thoughts of many hearts will be revealed. And a sword will pierce your own soul too" (Luke 2:22-35).

It would be fair to say that, with the thoughts and experiences that Mary had already had regarding this uncommon Son of hers, no person has ever contemplated the meaning of the life of Jesus with more depth than she did.

Twelve years later, the anxiety of Joseph and Mary over this eldest Son of theirs was magnified greatly. One cannot help wondering about the type of discipline that Joseph and Mary exercised over their children. Without doubt, by this time their family had grown to include several other children (see Matthew 13:55-56). Certainly, obedience to parental authority was not only expected, but was carried out in Joseph's household.

On this particular occasion, however, it seems that the temple elders took things into their own hands and decided to keep Jesus at the temple without telling His parents. He was there to discuss with the elders the meaning of the Passover and their common faith. His family expected Him to return to Nazareth with them and their relatives.

Plainly, this action was wrong for *any* reason as far as His parents were concerned, and we can hardly imagine Mary and Joseph taking this matter lightly. They had gone a day's journey from Jerusalem, and after discovering that Jesus was not with their relatives or friends as they had supposed, they searched their caravan for *three days*, working their way back toward Jerusalem. Runaway children were not known in Joseph's household. Obviously, as is indicated in Luke 2:44-45, many in their clan probably searched too.

But crime was known in Jerusalem. Had He been abducted? Had He been molested or killed, the victim of a heinous act by some of the hoodlums who came to create trouble each year when the crowds had gathered for Passover? Only those loving parents who have had their own child missing would be able to fully understand the wrenching agony of such an ordeal, and that would be indescribable even as it is true in our times!

For the first few hours after discovering that Jesus was missing, Joseph was probably consumed with righteous anger. He was a just man who took his parenting responsibilities very seriously. But Mary's anxiety certainly turned quickly to a deep fear of the worst. It is at times such as this that one prays in desperation, and when no answer comes, either good or bad, the desperation turns to despair.

Mary—contemplative and devout woman though she was—could not pray with faith, but only fright. Joseph—practical, settled and organized though he was —became emotionally distraught, determining more than ever to keep on looking. "We can't give up," He told Mary. "Maybe we can still find Jesus alive if we just keep looking."

They drove themselves beyond exhaustion. "Can't eat much. Can't sleep much. Where is He? What has happened to Him?" This continued on for three days.

They fully expected to find Him in the sleazy part of the big city, held by someone who wanted to use Him for some unholy purpose. After searching that area with no results, they finally decided there was only one place left to look—the temple. Inquiring at every doorway they passed, they described Jesus over and over again. When their hope was all but gone, they met a temple servant who told them he had seen such a lad in the elders' chambers.

Never would they have expected to find Jesus still in the temple with a group of supposedly responsible elders and teachers. Surely these temple leaders should have had enough sense to either return the boy to His family caravan or arrange with His parents for Him to stay for advanced instruction. Could it be possible they were so insensitive to His family's feelings? Didn't they have families of their own? One of the most severe disillusionments a person can experience is that of being let down, especially by those from whom one should be able to expect at least minimal, if not reasonable, responsibility.

Running into the temple complex, exhausted and desperate, Joseph and Mary banged on the door to the room. Normally, reverent quietness might be found in this part of the temple, but all eyes in that corridor were abruptly attracted to this anxious couple.

19

An elder opened the door with impatient anger, but Joseph, seeing Jesus inside, charged past him, nearly knocking him to the floor, and Mary followed. No time for protocol.

Seeing Jesus in such a situation, Joseph was overwhelmed by confusing emotions. On the one hand he wanted to hug his Son, but on the other hand he felt that he ought to spank Him. One or the other, and maybe even both. But which one first?

Mary, when she hugged Him as though He had just returned from the dead, could only whisper, "My Boy is safe. Thank God, my Boy is safe!"

Gaining some presence of mind after a few minutes, Joseph looked around at the irritated, angered faces of the scholars in the room. With fiery rage in his eyes, he lashed out at them for keeping their Son at the temple without first getting his approval. These pious religionists were not accustomed to having a peasant, especially one from Galilee, speak to them in such harsh tones, but Joseph could have cared less.

Mary, bending down to Jesus asked, "Son, why have you treated us like this? Your father and I have been anxiously searching for You" (Luke 2:48).

One of the elders interrupted. "We have found your Boy to be unusually well versed in the Law and the Prophets. He has listened to our instruction and has been asking us questions that show deep insight. He has given answers to our questions with outstanding comprehension. There is little doubt that He will become a gifted leader one day." Obviously, Jesus was receiving instruction well. (A popular painting depicts the boy Jesus teaching the elders, but the biblical account does not indicate that this is what was happening.)

Joseph, still trying to regain his composure after this ordeal, ordered Jesus and Mary out of the room. He followed without a further word or even a backward glance, slamming the door behind him.

Luke tells us that Jesus returned home to Nazareth with His parents and was obedient to them. The peculiar statement that he expressed to Mary and Joseph in the temple, "Didn't you know I had to be in My Father's house?" (Luke 2:49) might have been something for Mary to think about, but Joseph had other thoughts. Jesus continued to grow in both stature and wisdom from the combination of His parents' discipline and love, and the ever-present care of His heavenly Father.

+ + + + +

Sometime during the next eighteen years, Joseph apparently died. Jesus, being the eldest son, would have had the responsibility of the family's care from the time Joseph was disabled until the time when the next eldest son, probably James, could carry it.

Though Jesus would have had ultimate oversight of His mother as long as He and she were alive, the next eldest brother probably took over the task of family support once Jesus reached about thirty years of age. This would have left Him free to carry out the ministry for which He was destined.

Soon after Jesus' ministry began, He and His mother, Mary, and the rest of their family were invited to attend a wedding in Cana, a small town not far from Nazareth. Mary now realized that Jesus was ready to start fulfilling what she knew was His appointed work.

Perhaps Jesus, as a young rabbi, had taken part in the wedding ceremony with the local priest. But after the ceremony, the feast got underway. The guests enjoyed the food and wine, drinking up the best aged wine first, then consuming all of the lesser quality wine. But the evening was still young. Jesus' friends had come too, and none of the guests were ready to go home yet. Word got to Mary that the host, probably the bride's father, was embarrassed that the wine was gone. Mary assured him, "I'll see what I can do."

She went to the table where Jesus sat. She said to Him, "Jesus, come with me for a minute. I have to talk to you alone." Excusing Himself, He went outside with her. "The servants are out of wine. Is there anything you can do?" she inquired.

"I can ask some of my friends to look around town to see if they can find any," He replied almost in a whisper. "No, No. There isn't time," Mary responded.

"Our host is very nervous and humiliated, Jesus. I know what was told to me by the messenger from God before You were born. You could meet this need right here if You would—You know You can," Mary urged.

"Mother, My time isn't yet. Don't push Me. I'm not ready for that." Mary, quietly but firmly held her ground. "Jesus, when is the right time? When are you going to fulfill God's purpose? He determines the time, doesn't He?"

Mary's penetrating questions couldn't be argued, and Jesus then knew that the time had come for His ministry to begin. They both returned to the room She instructed the servants to go to Him, which they did. Jesus told them what to do (John 2:4-11). With His first miracle, the evening's finest wine was produced. This provided the first public verification that Jesus was the uniquely begotten Son of the Creator God. Up until that time, only Mary and Jesus were aware of what this meant.

Mary was the instrument of God in the supernatural birth of Jesus into the world. She was also instrumental in the birth of His supernatural miracles and ministry.

+ + + + +

Mary and the rest of Jesus' family followed His ministry with more than common interest. Some of His adventures were occasions for great family pride, some for grave concern for His safety, some for doubts as to whether He really was who He said He was, and some for deep heart rending sorrow.

On one occasion, Mary may have been perplexed, not knowing how to take one of His declarations. It was at one of Jesus' preaching stops, when He had gone to the home of a sympathetic believer who lived near Lake Galilee. Word got out to the general public that Jesus was there. By this time His reputation as a miracle-working teacher from Nazareth was widespread. A crowd comprised of curiosity seekers, believers, hero worshipers and doubting skeptics soon gathered in front of the house. As many as knew the owner had come inside. Soon the doorways were jammed. Jesus tried to be heard as best He could.

Outside, a commotion took place. Jesus' mother and His brothers had made their way through the throng as far as the door of the house, but could go no farther. In frustration, one of His brothers had tapped the shoulder of a fellow just inside the door and asked him to tell Jesus right away that His mother wanted to see Him. The message was relayed to Jesus.

He may have been a bit irritated that His teaching was so abruptly interrupted. Or, more likely, He may have come to a conclusion in His talk about how the Heavenly Father regards the high place His human creation holds in His affection. Perhaps Jesus realized that a golden opportunity to illustrate His message had presented itself by this unexpected appearance of His closest relations.

He seized the opportunity. "You ask Me how I can call the God of Israel My Heavenly Father? I will tell you. I have just been told that my mother and brothers want to talk to Me. You see, as God is My Heavenly Father, so also all of you who have faith and believe in Me will be as close to Him as if you were My brothers and sisters, and even My mother. Does this help you to understand how much your Heavenly Father cares for you?" (Matthew 12:46-56)

Would a mother want others to think that they could be as close to her Son as she is? Certainly Mary pondered this in her heart. Let us realize that she didn't have 2,000 years of analysis to evaluate Jesus' words, as we do; the actions of Christ were just happening. What Mary's Son was teaching had never before been heard by His listeners.

How could anyone think that He could be that close to God? How could anyone claim to be a son or a daughter to the God of Abraham, Isaac and Jacob? Was this blasphemy? Mary had a right, as any mother does, to feel that until her Son marries, she would be first in His heart. She felt that she had not yet understood all that His declaration meant.

+ + + + +

The agony at the foot of the cross of Jesus has been recorded by the four Gospel writers. All agree that Mary, His mother, was there. There was nothing anyone could do that would comfort her. No uprising against the system which allowed such gross miscarriages of justice could salve the unspeakable misery of her heart. She had loved her eldest Son, this Child of the seed of God, with a love that knew no bounds. Gladly would she have traded places with Him, but she knew that could never be.

Her mind whirled in turmoil over the events of the past thirty-three years. Standing in the temple with her beloved Joseph, holding her infant Son in her arms, the old prophet Simeon had predicted what was now coming to pass (Luke 2:34-35). The spear that pierced the side of Jesus pierced Mary's soul at the same time. We may wonder how she ever lived through that horror.

While on the cross, Jesus, being fully aware of the depth of His mother's agony, had to set one more affair in order. As long as He was alive, He was ultimately responsible for His mother's care. So He turned over that task to His youngest disciple, John, possibly because His brothers had by this time left home as well. From our viewpoint, it would look like the choice couldn't have been better. But from the viewpoint of the people who knew him, the choice of John couldn't have been worse.

Jesus knew the deepest chambers of the hearts of both His mother and this most disliked of all His disciples. He also knew that Mary still had something to teach about how to love, and John had something he desperately needed to learn about how to love. The New Testament later shows how well she taught and how well John learned (see Chapter 7).

A little over fifty days after the crucifixion, Mary sat in a room in Jerusalem with about 120 other people (Acts 1:14-15). Oh, what they had seen in those fifty days! Though Jesus had died on the cross and some of them had witnessed it, they saw Him again, alive with the wounds of the nails and the spear quite evident. He had risen again to life by His own power!

When she first heard of this wonder, Mary readily believed it to be true. She knew, as no one else in that room apparently knew, how Jesus had been born. Only Matthew and Luke refer to Jesus' miraculous birth. Since their Gospels were written several years after Jesus' ascension to Heaven, Mary must have finally revealed to these two writers what had happened. She now understood that Jesus' ultimate verification of His divine mission was to be His resurrection from the dead, even more than in His miraculous birth or ministry.

As she put all of Jesus' life together within her mind, Mary also knew that His greatest influence had not yet been made known. Her joy at Jesus' resurrection could not be described. Though He was no longer with her, the very fact that He was alive and had ascended to the Presence of the God who had placed Him within her thirty-three years earlier, produced a joy adequate enough to replace the days of agony and sorrow that had plagued her recent life.

Suddenly, along with the others in that room, Mary witnessed yet one more birth—the birth of the Church. At Jesus' own birth, there had been the visit of the shepherds telling of the angels' announcement and their heavenly song. Later, the wise men from the East told her and Joseph of the star they followed which led them to Bethlehem.

Now, however, Mary was seeing the wonders of a supernatural phenomenon for herself: the sound like a rushing mighty wind, the flashing tongues like fire, each touching every person there. Their excitement and joy were unimaginable! Now the promised Holy Spirit had come to stay with them. Before her own eyes, Mary was witnessing the result of her Son's true work and ministry, and it was marvelous to behold! (Acts 1 and 2)

+ + + + +

The highest calling in life that God gives women is the implanting of themselves into the lives of their children, though some may find satisfaction in other achievements, too. Perhaps this is a woman's highest calling because it calls forth the most from what a woman really can be.

Looking at the life of this queen of mothers, one would probably never wish to trade places with her, even considering her eternal honor. More was demanded of her in humility, wisdom, grace, long-suffering, patience, and all of the most noble and desired virtues than anyone else would ever be expected to achieve.

Yet, in some measure, God now brings them forth in all who are wholly committed to Christ as Lord of their life. You may wonder how you could possibly endure suffering through weeks or months of agony, illness or deprivation. You may pray that you never have to find out.

You will not be called upon to answer that question in advance, for no one really knows what they can do until they must do it. God knows, however, and that is good enough; for He holds all the events of your life—short-term and long-term, good and bad, easy and hard—safely in His hands.

Chapter 3

Herod:
A Tyrannical Genius

An encounter with Jesus Christ causes reactions in people that are unpredictable. They may vary from being born into a whole new creation of the spirit to a radical or reactionary rebellion against anything or anyone who represents righteousness, decency, honor or the Christian faith itself. Either may happen with king or commoner, for both are human.

The world has known many tyrants, some who have become major historical figures, and some who have left us only the effects of the misery they created. One such tyrant was Herod the Great.

The various tyrants recorded in our history books often illustrated some quality of human achievement that revealed their great potential for the benefit of the world. But because of their twisted and depraved values, they have illustrated how such an attribute can be used to bring chaos, suffering, starvation and eventually the demise of their own evil rule. Such was the reign of Herod.

Some of these despots were dynamic personalities with the ability to forcefully persuade their unthinking subjects to follow them blindly, come what may. Saddam Hussein, Hitler, Stalin, Mussolini, Kaiser Wilhelm II, and Napoleon Bonaparte fit such a description. They were all possessed by a ruthless determination to satisfy their evil lust for power. They were able to command multitudes of people who obeyed them without hesitation out of fear of the conscienceless reprisal that would come against them or their loved ones. Such were the tactics of Herod.

Some tyrants were inheritors of positions of power already long established before them, and merely by the accident of their birthright were thrust upon the world scene. Often these men, and some women too, have been psychopathic murderers, bathed in lustful debauchery, whose only goal in life was to maintain or increase the power of their throne until they died of old age. Whatever blood had to be spilled in expanding the boundaries of their domain was of no consequence to them. These despots considered that the "divine right of kings" to rule was of more importance than the responsibility of people to rule themselves under God, "with liberty and justice for all." Such was the attitude of Herod.

It has only been in the past two centuries that the political doctrine that governments are to be the servants of the people has spread throughout the world, beyond the shores of a very new kind of nation. It was "conceived in liberty, and dedicated to the proposition that all men are created equal..." and their government should be "of the people, by the people, and for the people..." (Abraham Lincoln's Gettysburg Address).

When we consider the name of Herod, we cannot limit it to merely one man. It was actually a family name of six generations of rulers of Israel. The birth of Jesus Christ occurred around the middle of the rule of this dynasty. The Herods ruled only by permission and appointment from Caesar. They were not Romans, and neither were they Jews by either blood, faith or practice. They were of Idumean (Southern Israel) descent. The name Herod stands for "heroic," but certainly didn't describe them.

Over the years of their rule, this dynasty accumulated considerable power. They knew how to use it, even to the extent of carrying out what appears to us to be incomprehensible slaughters. In theory they were only allowed to commit such acts with Roman permission. This was sometimes overlooked, however, since the Herods had become successful tax collectors for Rome. Such death decrees had become a way of life with them whenever there was even the hint of a threat to either their own power or to that of Rome.

Jesus was born during the reign of the third Herod of this dynasty, who had inherited not only the throne of Galilee, but some of the qualities and the debauchery of his father, Herod Antipater I, who considered himself a king. This tyrant was killed by an assassin while serving as the appointed governor of Judea.

This third Herod, who chose to name himself Herod the Great, was his father's second oldest son. He caused the name of Herod to be feared and even dreaded, but never revered. He was a tyrant who combined ruthless leadership with inherited power. He was a genius as an architect and built magnificent cities in honor of Caesar, thereby increasing his own power and influence as an agent of Rome.

Herod the Great was in Rome at the time of his father's assassination. Having gained the favor of the Emperor Anthony, he was immediately appointed to his father's position as "King of Judea" when only 25 years old. In order to secure his position there, he forced himself upon the people of Jerusalem, which had been taken over by his older brother, Phaseal. When Phaseal learned that the position had been given to his brother, he committed suicide. He knew what to expect from his jealous younger brother.

The position of Jewish high priest was at that time conferred by the king. During his reign, Herod appointed Aristobulus, his brother-in-law, to that honor, but he soon felt threatened by him and had him killed. Because of this, his wife, Mariamne, who was only one of Herod's several wives and was the only one he really loved, turned against him. Sensing that she too was becoming a threat, and still being held in favor by the emperor of Rome, Herod murdered her along with his own two sons born to her. To expand his rule, in a war with the Arabians to the south, Herod totally crushed them. Since there were relatives in his household that were related to them, he ordered their deaths as well.

Such were the ways of this psychopathic tyrant, who by this time was only about thirty years old. He later executed more of his sons by other wives whom he considered to be plotting against him.

In total contrast, it would seem Herod the Great did make significant contributions to the culture of the Jewish nation. By brutal force, he rid the land to a large extent of the highway robbers who had plagued the commercial roadways for many years. He established peace in the land, too, but showed no mercy to anyone threatening rebellion or revolution. He did this, of course, with the blessing of Rome. Under such oppressive rule, the citizenry had only one choice—to make sure they did nothing to upset the King.

Herod did, however, accomplish several things that made both the Romans and the Jews happy, and in these things he proved himself the master tactician. He displayed uncommon political talent, which was far superior to that of his brothers, whom he soon overshadowed. He knew men, especially those of influence even to the Emperor, and he knew how to use them to accomplish his own desires.

Rome loved power, prestige and money. Herod learned that by conquering other lands, by annihilating any opposition and by collecting generous taxes for Rome, he could secure his position, even if it meant relying mostly on shrewd, clandestine and devious methods. He had no friends, but he also had no open enemies. He was, therefore, able to maintain his position for a generation.

Herod was also a master architect, and has been compared favorably with the ancient Pharaohs of Egypt. The ruins of a magnificent theatre and amphitheater built by Herod still stand in Jerusalem. It was Herod who introduced the pious Jews to the frivolity and gayety of the Greek and Roman cultures. This angered the orthodox Jews, who viewed this as an insult to their most sacred principles of life and religion.

This opposition is probably what led Herod to set out on his most acclaimed work. He rebuilt the holiest place of the Jewish faith, the temple in

Jerusalem, which originally had been built by King Solomon, the son of the great King David. Herod's temple was described by the Jewish historian Josephus as being more magnificent than Solomon's, and indeed it became regarded as one of the wonders of the world.

One part of it still remains—the Wailing Wall—which is Judaism's most sacred shrine today. Even after years of reconstruction, the temple was not yet finished at the time Jesus was born. It was finally completed after Herod's death, shortly before Jesus began His ministry at the age of thirty.

Herod also built temples in Samaria, a northern province inhabited by intermarried Caananitish Jews, but whom the Jews of Judea hated and considered to be half-breeds. He then built a harbor where there was none before, which astounded the world because this phenomenon was considered impossible. Herod also constructed three huge towers there in honor of his relatives, including his wife, Mariamne, whom he had executed. He built the city of Caesarea in honor of the Emperor. He also built major edifices in cities well beyond the borders of his own jurisdiction, such as Damascus, Tripoli, Tyre, Sidon (now in Lebanon) and even in Athens.

Yet Herod is remembered most vividly for only one act, which was accomplished with lightning terror. A group of traveling astrologers from the East (called "wise men" in Matthew's Gospel) told him of the birth of a new "king of the Jews." Many historians believe that these men came from Persia, now known as Iran. Even in his old age, Herod was insanely jealous. When he inquired of these astrologers and the temple scholars as to where this Child was to be born, they read him the prophecy foretelling the birth of Jesus in Bethlehem. He cunningly told the astrologers to go to Bethlehem. Once they had found the Child, they were to return and let him know where this King was, that he might go and "honor" Him, too.

Without doubt, Herod sent sleuths to track these honored guests of his country, in order to locate this new threat to his position. Though his lifestyle was hardly in conformity to the teachings of the Jewish Scriptures, he nevertheless reverenced these writings to some degree. When it was revealed to him that this Child, so strangely born to commoner parents in Bethlehem, had long before been predicted in Holy Writ, Herod chose to believe it without question. He certainly was not looking for a Savior of Israel, however, for he regarded himself as this. As far as he was concerned, any competitor must be "wasted."

It was astounding to Herod to hear these wise men tell of a mysterious star which was leading them to this new King. They seemed so certain that it was His star (Matthew 2:2). Matthew gives no indication as to what convinced these men of this star's significance or what induced them to mount their camels or horses and follow its movements. None of the other Gospels mention this episode. Possibly a messenger of God had spoken to them as he had spoken to Mary, Joseph and the shepherds.

Apparently Herod and his cohorts couldn't see that star. Otherwise why would it have been necessary for crafty old Herod to ask the temple scholars where all this was to take place? Certainly he could have searched the skies for himself. The astrologers saw the star shining over the place where the Holy Child lay. Bethlehem is located only six miles from Jerusalem to the south. One can imagine that Herod's uncontrollable rage was triggered by this frustration of not knowing how to find this child for himself. This was coupled with the fact that, as the Jewish historian Josephus tells us, Herod in his old age was suffering from the advanced stages of incurable venereal disease. This was increasingly robbing him of whatever rational judgment he still might have had. In his prime, Herod had possessed unusual physical strength and a brilliant intellect.

Herod now felt only the soul-possessing power of his jealousy. He proceeded to act under its control. He ordered that every first-born male child in Bethlehem under two years of age be butchered without mercy by his militia. Herod did this after being told that the astrologers, aware of his treacherous schemes, had returned to the East without reporting back to him. This indicates that the wise men did not visit Jesus at the manger, but in a house

(Matthew 2:11), possibly as long as two years after His birth.

It had been only a year or two before this heinous act that Herod had executed his wife and his two sons. This prompted Emperor Augustus in Rome to exclaim, "I would rather be Herod's hog than his son." In deference to the Jews Herod did not eat pork.

Thanks to a divine warning in another of Joseph's dreams, Mary and Joseph were able to escape from Herod's massacre with Jesus and flee to Egypt. Joseph's absolute submission to God's instructions is shown by the fact that he acted immediately and without debating with God. Joseph and Mary had been charged with the care, custody and rearing of this holy Child, and the urgency of the angel's message in the dream was apparent. Joseph took them and went stealthily out of the city. Possibly even as Herod's death squads were coming into Bethlehem from the north, Joseph, Mary and Jesus were leaving heading south.

The family remained in Egypt for about two years or until Herod was dead. Jesus would have been about four years old then. Joseph had learned that the messages God's angel delivered through dreams were a vital necessity for the protection of his little family. This time, he was ordered to return to Israel, but to bypass Judea in secret because of the new ruler Archelaus, Herod's equally tyrannical son.

They were to continue on to Nazareth in Galilee, which was to be their permanent home.

What an adventure! Joseph had only been expecting to pay his taxes in Bethlehem; yet he ended up being gone from his home for at least four years. All of this was caused by one mad genius-tyrant, whom Joseph had probably never seen or met, much less ever wanted to meet.

"Evil has within itself the seeds of its own destruction." This time-proven proverb comes to us full force in the example set by Herod the Great. The same was passed on to his sons and grandsons, with the possible exception of Herod Agrippa II, who more than forty years later was almost persuaded by St. Paul to become a Christian (Acts 25:13—26:32).

When Herod the Great heard of the young Child who had been predicted to be the king of the Jews, he allowed all of the vile forces of evil within him to come into play at once. This produced the only significant act of his life for which he is best remembered—"the slaughter of the innocents" in Bethlehem.

Some believe that no matter how bad we might be, the good in us will balance off the bad, for man is inherently good. The end result of Herod's life illustrates the opposite, however. Herod's most acclaimed beneficial achievement was the rebuilding of the temple in Jerusalem, which took nearly fifty years to complete. Yet only a few years later in 70 A.D., the forces of Rome to which Herod had shown such loyalty ransacked Jerusalem, utterly demolishing that magnificent structure so that only one foundation wall remains.

On his second missionary journey, the apostle Paul traveled north from Jerusalem through some of the cities outside Israel where Herod had built magnificent structures. Though the destruction of Jerusalem had not yet occurred, upon his arrival in Galatia (in central Turkey) Paul may well have thought of Herod's wretched death. Some years later he wrote a letter to the Galatian Church, which he sent from Rome, the city to which Herod was so loyal. In it Paul wrote, "Do not be deceived: God cannot be mocked. A man reaps what he sows. The one who sows to please his sinful nature, from that nature will reap destruction..." (Galatians 6:7-8).

Herod encountered his greatest crisis when he perceived the infant Jesus as a threat to his power. He let his overwhelming jealousy drive him to commit a barbarous massacre.

Regardless of the pattern of life one lives, an encounter with Jesus Christ will above all other crises call for a life-determining decision. Like Herod, that crisis may well bring forth the worst of what each of us is capable of being. Or it may bring forth the best of what God can make us. But that encounter can never be taken lightly or ignored.

Chapter 4

John the Baptist: A Rugged Individualist

Surely there will never again be anyone like John the Baptist. As is said of some, "after they made him, they threw the mold away." John the Baptist could only have done what he did in the way he did it if God's Spirit were uniquely upon him.

As the people of John's day discovered, though he was indeed strange, this man was anything but crazy. What he preached out in the wilderness along the Jordan River made a lot of sense. Repenting for sin, seeking God's forgiveness, making restitution, and being baptized as a sign of resolve to do all this—that's a mighty strong proclamation. Yet as the forerunner of the ministry of Jesus Christ, it cost him his life.

No one had preached like John, since Amos, the sheepherder-prophet from Tekoa, who lived more than seven hundred years before. And John the Baptist feared no one. He wasn't preaching in anyone else's territory. The people were coming to him, so he said what needed to be said. If some of his listeners didn't like it, they would have to live with that problem. Judging by the fact that his reputation spread like wildfire in dry grass, for many their "problem" must have gone back home with them, for there certainly developed strong feelings regarding him.

About thirty years earlier, this Jordan River preacher had been born into a devout Jewish home to gentle parents who weren't expected to have any children. Elizabeth, his mother, had passed beyond her child-bearing years wishing for a child, but had remained barren. Zacharias, his father, at one time fully intending to have a family like any Jewish priest or rabbi, had grown more discouraged as the years passed. And now, long since burned out, this middle-aged couple had settled down in hopelessness, resigned to their fate of sterility on the part of either or both of them. This was most disheartening for them, for in those times it was a woman's highest honor to bear a son, and a man's highest honor to claim a son.

Though the practice was not uncommon, Zacharias was not willing to divorce Elizabeth and trade her for another woman who might bear him a son. It became his resolve that, childless or not, he loved her too much to reject her, and her devotion to him likewise was complete. At that time, this faithful couple was ministering to the needs of a small congregation in the back hill country of Judea, undoubtedly expecting to finish their active years there. However, according to the system of the priests, Zacharias was required to go to the temple in Jerusalem each year to minister in a rotation of "divisions." By casting lots, one priest of the division on duty was chosen to offer the incense at the proper time. Zacharias had undoubtedly done this before, and when the lot fell to him, he expected that the ceremony would be routine.

But this time when he entered behind the sacred curtain to make the offering on the altar of incense, he was confronted by an exceedingly bright angel standing to the right of the altar. Zacharias was too frightened to move. Who did he know that had ever seen an angel before? He had read of something like this happening to Isaiah the Prophet (Isaiah 6), but why would an angel of God appear to this unimportant country priest? He certainly didn't figure, especially at his age, that he was qualified to be any Isaiah.

Suddenly the strange divine intruder began to speak, and only Zacharias could hear him. (We don't know whether he ever got around to offering the incense or not.) The angel calmed him down by telling him he had nothing to fear. He told him that God had heard the many quiet prayers that he and

Elizabeth had offered for so long, though they now had given up hope of getting them answered. Elizabeth, he told the priest, would at long last bear a son, but his son was destined for a distinct purpose by God Himself. He was to drink no wine, and he was to be filled with God's Spirit in a unique way from birth. He would cause many in Israel to repent and return to God as Elijah had done centuries before, and he would prepare the people for the coming of the long-promised Messiah.

Zacharias had no idea what the angel meant by the last statement about preparing the people for the Messiah. But at that moment he was sure the angel must have made a mistake, or else arrived to tell him all this considerably too late. Him? He and Elizabeth couldn't have children now, and surely the angel could see the wrinkled face and the thinning gray hair on his head. "How can I be sure of this? I am an old man and my wife is well along in years," he questioned (Luke 1:18).

The angel then introduced himself in no uncertain terms. "I am Gabriel. I stand in the presence of God, and I have been sent to speak to you and to tell you this good news. And now you will be silent and not able to speak until the day this happens, because you did not believe my words, which will come true at their proper time" (Luke 1:19-20).

Normally, the offering of the incense did not take very long. The crowd of worshipers waited outside the curtain and continued in prayer. But after the usual time had elapsed, some began to raise their eyes and look for Zacharias to come out. The curtain didn't move.

Gradually a low murmur arose, some thinking that perhaps he had taken ill while in there; possibly he had experienced a stroke or a heart attack. Two or three other priests, fearing the worst, moved toward the curtain to investigate. Just then it slowly parted.

There stood Zacharias as if he were just recovering from amnesia. After so long a time the people wondered if he even remembered they were there. Certainly something, perhaps a vision they thought, had held him in there for so long, for he was unable to utter a word. Through a sort of impromptu sign language, he directed that the ceremonies proceed. Other priests stepped in to finish his duties.

Elizabeth was aware that something almost beyond description happened to her husband that day. Only able to describe in writing what had occurred, she read his words and gasped at what was on the tablet. The couple traveled home together in deep contemplation. Such a revelation is not quickly absorbed.

When they got home, Zacharias took Elizabeth in his arms as he had done so many times before. But there seemed to be a warmth between them that neither had felt for years. He caressed her face, which seemed to have lost the lines of time, and her skin again seemed soft, glowing and young. The fire of youthful passion returned for this glorious and miraculous moment, and the love of these two faithful companions-for-life was sealed as they again became one.

Elizabeth's ecstasy at the birth of her son knew no bounds. He was strong and healthy, and the aged mother nursed him as though she were a young woman with the joy of her fondest dream fulfilled.

The custom of the Jews was that a boy was officially named on the eighth day after his birth, at the sacred ceremony of circumcision. This was the sign that a Jewish boy had become an heir of the covenant made between God and Abraham, and all the generations of Abraham's posterity. Through this promise, God was to make of them a nation that would bless the world.

All of the relatives and neighbors who had gathered for this event assumed that the baby would be named after his father, since he was Zacharias' firstborn son. But Elizabeth told them that his name was to be John. This was a name that no one else among all their relatives had. Surely Zacharias would not tolerate this insult to his name. But when they asked him as he came into the room, Zacharias called for a tablet, since he was still unable to speak after more than nine months. To their astonishment, he wrote, "His name is John" (Luke 1:63).

Immediately his speech returned, and the pent up joy and praise to God that he had been unable to express seemed to flow out all at once in a flood.

John was about six months old when Jesus, his cousin, was born. Without doubt they saw each other and played together whenever the two families visited.

As he grew into adulthood, John decided to take the sacred vow of a Nazarite. (This had nothing to do with the town of Nazareth.) This was a deeply religious, personal vow to voluntarily set himself apart from the common life to the service of God alone.

In the Old Testament, there were several short-term Nazarites, who performed some special work of God. The vow was usually not for more than one hundred days duration. The only ones we know of who were Nazarites for life were the Israelite judge, Samson (Judges 13:24—16:31), the prophet Samuel, and John the Baptist. Women could become Nazarites too, but the Bible does not name any.

For the short-termer, the hair was to be entirely shaved off at the time the vow was taken, and it was not to be cut until the time of service had been fulfilled. Then it was shaved off again, and the cut hair was burned as a sign that the sacred duties had been completed.

To become a Nazarite, a person had to vow:

1. To strictly abstain from wine or any product of the vine.

2. To never cut or trim the hair or beard.

3. To refrain from touching any dead body.

4. To not eat any unclean food or meat (Judges 13:5-7; Numbers 6).

St. Paul took the Nazarite vow at least once for a limited period of time, and he completed his term with some other early Christians (Acts 18:18; 21:23-26).

Apparently it was common knowledge among the Jews that John the Baptist was a Nazarite. This gave him a voice of authority that he otherwise would not have had, for the Nazarite vow was similar to the vows taken at the ordination of a Jewish priest.

At some point in his life, probably after both his father and mother had died, John came to live in the wilderness lands of Judea, near the southern end of the Jordan River. He loved this wild land, which he learned to literally live off. He was dependent upon no one, and no one was dependent upon him. His only companions were the creatures of the desert and God Himself.

One wonders how John became so well acquainted with the religious stagnation, the corruption of sin in the people, and the need for their repentance. Surely God did His own tutoring of John, preparing him for his divinely appointed ministry. Possibly

John's lifestyle enabled him to learn better than those who lived within the flow of society.

By preaching to those who passed along the trade route running from Jerusalem to Jericho and on to areas in the east, John's reputation spread rapidly.

Curiosity drove some to come out to hear this "wild man" and to see his strange baptisms. But when Jesus came to be baptized, John apparently knew that this phase of his work was nearing an end, for he urged his followers to listen to and believe in Jesus, which many of them subsequently did.

John's message was respected throughout the land, even to the extent that those who opposed him dared not silence him. Thousands of people, including some of the highest officials of the temple and the government, were fiercely loyal to him.

King Herod Antipas, son of Herod the Great, ruled a province northeast of Judea. Though he didn't like what John said, he still felt compelled to hear him. Undoubtedly this was the closest he ever got to changing his bloody, treacherous and immoral pattern of life.

One day John went too far, however. Why did he have to get personal in his condemnation of Herod's sin? He could flay away at the sins of the rabble all he wanted to, but a wise preacher does not speak against the king. To his face, John had condemned

Herod for marrying Herodias, the wife of his brother Philip, after an adulterous relationship.

Herod decided that John must be silenced, though he was afraid to put him to death. The king feared the prophet because he knew he was righteous and holy. He was also concerned about an uprising among the vast throng in the land who were so intensely loyal to John; so he put John in prison, but he kept him safe and continued to listen to him (Mark 6:19-20).

One who has been free to wander, unattached and unencumbered for so many years, could not be imprisoned without having such confinement press deeply upon his emotions. In time, discouragement and doubt beset John like a black cloud, blurring his memory of the glorious days he once knew by the Jordan River. If he might have taken solace in the remembrance of the vast crowds on Jordan's shore, the hundreds of baptisms, his success in shaking the temple hierarchy to their shoes, John found none of it.

His most glorious memory was that of the baptism of Jesus and the descent of the Holy Spirit like a dove. This event stood as the high point of his entire life—even the fulfillment of his life's purpose.

But where was Jesus now? Why was He not here to minister to him in his hour of trial? Had he been deceived all this time? Perhaps Jesus was not the

Messiah after all. Had he baptized another forerunner instead of the true Messiah?

Herod had no intention of carrying out the censure of John more than merely by a prison exile, for Herod still liked him and allowed him visitors.

One day a few of John's devoted disciples came to visit him in prison. He asked these faithful friends to go out and find Jesus, wherever He might be, and ask Him if He was the Messiah, that he might satisfy his mind once and for all. He had heard about the miracles, the crowds, and the sermons Jesus had been preaching; but this nagging doubt, which plagued him like a growing cancer, had to be resolved lest he lose his mind.

John's disciples found Jesus soon, for His reputation had spread throughout the country. They joined the crowd around Him and gradually worked their way through it up to Jesus Himself. When they identified themselves and their mission, Jesus immediately inquired about John's welfare. When they told Him where John was and why he was there, Jesus was saddened to tears, for He also knew how slight a chance John would ever have to go free again.

Then came the great question from John's messengers. "Are you the one who was to come, or should we expect someone else?" (Matthew 11:1-3) Probably surprised and perplexed that John would wonder about this, Jesus turned and looked toward the crowd milling about. At first He thought He might explain to these inquirers what He was doing in His ministry, but then He changed His mind and decided to *show* them. Then they too could be eyewitnesses to all that was happening. Pointing out the healed and risen ones as He spoke, Jesus said to them, "Go back and report to John what you hear and see: The blind receive sight, the lame walk, those who have leprosy are cured, the deaf hear, the dead are raised, and the good news is preached to the poor. Blessed is the man who does not fall away on account of Me" (Matthew 11:4-6).

When He finished introducing those to whom He had ministered, Jesus spoke to the silent crowd about John the Baptist. Warning of the consequences for rejecting or ignoring the message of repentance that both John and He had preached, Jesus offered the ultimate answer of God to every person, "Come to Me, all who are weary and burdened, and I will give you rest. Take My yoke upon you and learn from Me, for I am gentle and humble in heart, and you will find rest for your souls. For My yoke is easy and My burden is light" (Matthew 11:28-30).

John's messengers returned to him and related all they had seen and heard. For the first time since his imprisonment John could rest from his doubts, for he now knew for certain that he had ordained the true Messiah.

Herod's primary problem in keeping John safe was in dealing with the hatred raging within the heart of his wife, Herodias. Herod had enticed her away from his brother, Philip, who ruled a province northeast of the Sea of Galilee.

Unlike her husband, Herodias had become consumed by a deep, bloodthirsty desire for revenge against John. She despised him for the insult of his public condemnation of her sin. But as long as Herod was in charge, she was powerless to order John's death. Unexpectedly she found an opportunity.

Herod frequently hosted lavish parties with plenty of wine, women and song. On this occasion, in celebration of his birthday, Herod as usual was well "juiced," but not to the point where he completely lost his head. His court dancers had done well in entertaining his guests, but he wanted to find someone to dance who was new and different from the others they had seen.

Maybe Herodias could do it. She had a classic figure and long, flowing black hair; but the undisciplined, spoiled life she had lived had taken its toll on her once beautiful skin and face. She was a little too intoxicated to be very graceful, anyway. Instead, Herodias suggested that her daughter by Philip, Salome, might please Herod. Of course! She was beautiful and graceful, just as Herodias used to be.

Herod sent a guard to Salome's quarters to summon her to the banquet hall. While he waited impatiently he called for more wine. The good wine had long since been consumed, so the poorer wine had to be brought in. But Herod didn't notice the difference by that time and neither did his guests.

Finally, Salome entered the hall. She was a sparkling vision of radiant beauty with gold, silver and jewels around her neck, arms, and ankles, and woven into her hair. Her gown was made of several softly draped lengths of shimmering, filmy cloth in shades of royal purple. It flowed behind her as she glided across the shiny marble floor. Her flowing raven hair finished the picture to perfection. As Herod saw this stunning vision standing before him, lithe and delightfully sensuous, he begged her to dance for them, with the applauding approval of every guest.

As the musicians began to play on their lyres, lutes and drums, the beat was slow and rhythmic. Salome began to dance hesitatingly, as if to make sure she was truly receiving the approval of the king and his guests. Herod would have none of this. He called out to her, "Loosen up, let's see what you can really do!" And he ordered the musicians to play at a faster tempo.

Salome threw herself into total abandon. She whirled and twirled, bending backward and forward, dancing across the floor in and out among the half-drunken guests. One man grabbed a part of her gown as she glided by. Soon other pieces of her dress were left among the roaring audience. With only one tiny piece of cloth left to cover her hips, she raced over to Herod who tried to grab it in his sweaty hands. She teasingly sprang out of his reach and ran to her mother, panting as her body glistened with tiny rivulets of perspiration. The crowd was in a lusting frenzy. Herod had slid off his couch onto the floor in exotic excitement, spilling his wine all over his royal bloated belly. Never had any girl electrified an audience like Salome.

Herod, with some help from his servants, clumsily picked himself up. He sank onto the couch and summoned Salome to come before him. She stood just beyond his reach, laughing enticingly.

Herod ordered the whistling, lecherous crowd to be silent. In thoughtless revelry he yelled, " 'Ask me for anything you want, and I'll give it to you.' And he promised her with an oath, 'Whatever you ask I will give you, up to half my kingdom' " (Mark 6:22-23).

There were many things a young woman of about twenty could have wanted, but half of Herod's arid, rock-strewn kingdom was not one of them. Puzzled by the generosity of the offer, she hesitated, then turned to her mother and motioned for her to go out of the hall with her to discuss what she should ask for. Amid the whistles and roars from the crowd lusting for more of the beautiful Salome, the two women stepped through the doors to a side room. "Mother, what shall I ask for?" Salome whispered. Herodias knew her answer immediately. What a perfect chance to accomplish what Herodias wanted most. She all but ordered Salome to ask for the Baptist's head. Though Salome didn't have the same intense hatred that her mother had, her desire was to please her mother, so she consented to ask for it, for John the Baptist meant nothing to her.

Together they entered the hall again amid a rising chorus of roars of approval from the guests. Salome stood before the king, still nearly nude to ensure his cooperation. The hall grew silent. Boldly, almost flippantly, she spoke: "I want you to give me right now the head of John the Baptist on a platter" (Mark 6:25).

The crowd gasped, and so did Herod. In the shock of her request and overlooking the vision of feminine perfection before him, he exclaimed, "Do you know what you are asking for, Salome? Do you know how the people feel about John? I may have an insurrection on my hands if I do that. Besides this, what has he ever done to you?" Salome looked at her mother as if she was not sure she should press for this request. But Herodias nodded back in defiant vengeance, for she was not going to let this opportunity escape her.

"Oh, King Herod." Salome spoke as a spoiled child coaxing candy from a parent. "You promised me my request before all your friends here. What would they think of a king who didn't keep his word?"

Herod, with his twisted sense of values, pondered this problem as much as his fuzzy, wine-sodden brain would allow. He looked across the stunned crowd. Then, after a long hesitation, with a wave of his hand he ordered his guards to carry out their heinous duty. They turned in reluctant obedience and marched out the door. The silence was broken only by their fading footsteps in the distant corridor.

It seemed like an eternity, but no one moved. Herod fell back on his couch and sobbed. Salome started to tremble as she saw the hardened look of bloodlust against John in her mother's eyes.

The sound of footsteps ascending from the lower stone staircase became louder as the guards approached the banquet hall. Every eye was turned toward the door. A murmur arose as it swung open and a soldier entered carrying a large, covered silver platter. He ran across the hall toward the table next to Herod where Salome and Herodias were now seated. The women guests shrieked in horror as the trembling guard set the platter on the table in front of Salome. She warily removed the lid and quickly pushed the platter in front of her mother. Many of the women fainted, falling into the arms of their escorts. Even some of the men ran groaning from the hall.

Salome gazed at the blood-spattered head with the long hair on the platter. She grew pale in horror as she began to realize what sort of favor she had asked. Then with her body still glistening from sweat, she slumped to the floor in a cold faint.

Herod gasped at this gruesome fulfillment of his promise. In the past when he had given orders to butcher anyone who even remotely threatened his rule, the executions were always carried out where he did not have to see them. He was unconcerned about how a human life may be valued. But what he was seeing now was more than he could bear. He hurriedly rose from his couch, held his hand over his mouth, and ran for his chambers, vomiting profusely as he crossed the hall, weaving and stumbling through the horror-stricken guests.

As Salome collapsed to the floor, her arm struck the platter, causing the head to roll off into the lap of Herodias. The blood of the Baptist splattered all over her royal finery, her arms and her hands. She hastily put the head back on the platter and attempted to wipe off the blood with a napkin. She only succeeded in spreading it the more, however. The feeling of John's blood on her hands seemed to be cold as ice, yet hot as fire. Herodias cringed, stood up, and swore at her daughter who had caused this soiling. She then stalked angrily out the door while still attempting, even more frantically, to wipe from her hands the blood she had so coldly demanded.

Word of this ghastly event spread throughout Israel like a gale. A public outcry demanded of Herod an answer as to why he had ordered John's death. Despite so many knowing the truth, he issued a statement saying that he had reason to fear that John was about to organize a rebellion against the government. But attempt to explain it as he would, the fact remained that John's blood cried out against the crowd's lust, Salome's sensuousness, Herod's debauchery, and Herodias' evil hatred in terms that none of Herod's explanations could ever conceal.

Herod later heard of the mighty works of Jesus and the throngs of people following Him. In a moment of panic, the whole gruesome event of his murder of the Baptist flashed before him again. "King Herod heard about this, for Jesus' name had become well known. Some were saying, 'John the Baptist has been raised from the dead, and that is why miraculous powers are at work in Him.' But when Herod heard this, he said, 'John, the man I beheaded, has been raised from the dead!' " (Mark 6:14-16)

When Jesus heard of John's death, He wanted His disciples to go with Him apart from the multitudes who followed them. He wept bitterly over the loss of one so dear. But then the realization came upon Him that no longer did He have a forerunner to share this ministry. John's words were now history. From that point on, Jesus stood alone.

+ + + + +

The life of John the Baptist was a crisis in itself. If he did not bring it, he lived it. He marked a historic turning point.

His life began through a divine miracle, but brought a crisis of faith to his mother and father. His ministry brought a crisis of judgment to a nation. His baptism of Jesus was the critical turning point toward the decline of his own work. And even in death, his blood brought an emotional and spiritual crisis of monumental proportions upon the king himself, and all who were with him at that fateful party.

It is amazing how profoundly one life can affect so many. John's message of judgment for sin and his call for repentance still comes to us today. The One for whom he was the forerunner completed the fulfillment of God's gracious promise of redemption. Now Jesus Christ brings to us the peace that ends the spiritual crisis for anyone who will gladly receive His gift of forgiveness, mercy and love.

Chapter 5

Nicodemus: A Puzzled Clergyman

Even a clergyman may have doubts about himself and his religious life. So what is it that causes a respected pillar of his community and society to begin re-examining his faith, all the way from his childhood training to his present life? One would not expect a renowned clergyman whose reputation for leadership and knowledge was well established to have to start all over again spiritually.

Nicodemus was by no means senile, neither was he so unsure of himself that he needed to go back to elementary school. It would seem that with all his vast learning, he had only succeeded in laying a foundation for what he really needed to learn. And it took two relatively unschooled men to show him what that was.

Knowledge consists of the accumulation in one's mind of facts. A person may be considered "learned" if he has stored up a great bank of facts on many subjects. Those who have done so are not necessarily considered wise, however, for wisdom is the ability to apply those facts to the greatest possible advantage for mankind in the most efficient way. If one were faced with having to choose between knowledge and wisdom—and since one does not create the other—it is best by far to choose wisdom, like King Solomon did (1 Kings 3:5-14).

Nicodemus was highly intelligent, a renowned teacher in Israel. But though his mind was full, his heart was empty. This drove him to Jesus in the middle of a quiet night to ask, to seek and to knock for some unknown answer. He neither knew what to ask, nor what it was that would be the right answer for which he sought.

It wasn't just a sudden impulse that thrust Nicodemus into the night in quest of an answer. There had been a rough-hewn, rude, volcanic preacher who had succeeded in shaking the hearts of thousands who had gone down to hear him by the muddy, winding Jordan River near the village of Bethany. This camel's-hair draped prophet had exploded onto the scene in Israel about 28 A.D., proclaiming the people's need to repent of injustices done against their neighbors and to be forgiven by God for their sins.

Nicodemus: A Puzzled Clergyman

To Nicodemus it was beyond comprehension why anyone would want to make that hot, uncomfortable journey from Jerusalem to the Jordan just to receive condemnation and verbal abuse heaped on him from this wilderness preacher, called John the Baptist, when he got there (Luke 3:7-14).

But go they did—by the thousands. So many went that this "wild man's" message began to disrupt the methodical, liturgical and sterile tranquility of the temple system of religion in Jerusalem. The people had been to hear John and had seen him call the repentant into the river to be bodily dipped under the water. Now they were persistently asking the temple teachers, Nicodemus among them, what this meant. It had gone past the point of ignoring this "baptizer" as a mere sensational upstart. He had to be checked out.

There is usually strength in numbers; so a group of the temple scholars, Nicodemus undoubtedly among them, made the miserable journey eastward. They had been convinced by previous scouting parties that they had better look into what was happening. They were particularly upset after they had discovered that Isaiah the Prophet had forecast the coming of such a strange messenger from God (Isaiah 40:3).

There was also another peculiar fact about this John the Baptist. It was no uncommon thing for the people of that time to be expecting the appearance of their long-awaited Messiah (God's Sent One). He was to come to set them free from the heel of Rome, which had trampled over them with such brutal force as they had not known since leaving their slavery in Egypt. A deliverer! Another Moses! When He came, the tables would indeed be turned, and the people of Israel would be free at last.

The hillsides near the Jordan had echoed the clear thundering voice of John as he proclaimed the Messiah, saying, "Repent, for the kingdom of heaven is near...I baptize you with water for repentance. But after me will come one who is more powerful than I, whose sandals I am not fit to carry. He will baptize you with the Holy Spirit and with fire..." (Matthew 3:2,11). Without doubt, Nicodemus heard this message.

Nicodemus stayed on through the next day. As before, several people stepped out of the crowd and walked to the river bank to await their turn to be baptized by John or one of his disciples. Standing close to the front of the crowd and staring at John, Nicodemus barely noticed a tall young Man, tanned and strong, quietly brush by him as He moved forward.

John raised the person whom he had finished baptizing and looked up to receive the next. John seemed to freeze in his movement. The appearance on his face indicated that something phenomenal was happening. Nicodemus looked back over his shoulder, then from side to side to see if there was something he was missing. He looked back to John who was slowly raising his arm and pointing to that bronzed young fellow who was now standing at the water's edge directly between Nicodemus and the Baptist. John seemed to be trembling as he stood waist deep in the water, leaning slightly against the current of the river.

"Will you baptize Me now, John?" Jesus asked quietly. John knew that the Messiah was coming, but he didn't know who He would be. Now, standing here before him was his own younger cousin, Jesus of Nazareth, whom he had known his entire life! Never had he dreamed that Jesus would be the One for whom he was the forerunner. But he sure knew it now!

Nicodemus and those around him stared transfixed at the drama unfolding before them. John, speaking as if he just came down from Mt. Sinai with Moses, cried out, "Look, the Lamb of God, who takes away the sin of the world! This is the one I meant when I said, 'A man who comes after me has surpassed me because He was before me.' I myself did not know Him, but the reason I came baptizing with water was that He might be revealed to Israel" (John 1:29-31). No, John had not known that Jesus was the One, but there was no doubt.

Lowering his voice so that only Jesus could hear, John protested that he should not baptize Him, but that he should be baptized by Jesus. John had baptized people as a sign that they had repented of their sins. How could God's Messiah be baptized for that?

Jesus replied, "Let it be so now; it is proper for us to do this to fulfill all righteousness" (Matthew 3:15). So John, with the silent crowd standing by, proceeded to baptize Jesus just as he had so many others before Him. Nicodemus was moved beyond words as he witnessed all this. After John had lifted Jesus up from the water, Jesus stopped, bowed His head and silently prayed.

Nicodemus was starting to bow silently too when he suddenly heard the flapping of wings. Even though there had been birds all around the bulrushes along the shore that day, he looked up in time to see a white dove fly toward Jesus and light on His head, where it remained while Jesus stood motionless.

After what seemed like several minutes, John called out to the people that it had been told him by divine revelation that one day he would baptize God's Messiah, and that He would be able to identify Him when he saw the Holy Spirit descend upon Him. Obviously, the Holy Spirit would have to be represented visibly in some way, and John knew that this dove was the symbol he waited for (John 1:33-34).

Just then a voice came out of Heaven. It wasn't loud and seemed to be directed only to Jesus and John. Nicodemus was unable to discern the words;

yet he knew instinctively that he was witnessing an event the like of which he would never see or hear again.

At the end of the day, Nicodemus returned to Jerusalem with the throng of people. Jesus was not among them, however, and He seemed to disappear from sight for several weeks.

Nicodemus was soon back at the routine of the temple and its prayers, hours, sacrifices, and religion as usual, except that now the students in his instruction classes were asking questions about this strange preacher down at the Jordan River. The memory of what he had seen would not leave him, nor did he want it to. Was he living in the actual time of the fulfillment of the prophecy of the Messiah, and in fact did he actually witness the ordination of Israel's Savior?

After a while word began to trickle into Jerusalem from travelers who had been north to the Province of Galilee that this Jesus was preaching and doing peculiar and mighty miracles among the people there. Nicodemus also heard that John the Baptist had been arrested and thrown into King Herod's prison east of the Dead Sea for speaking out against his marriage to his brother's wife, Herodias. Nicodemus thought to himself that John was either fearless or foolish, but that whichever he was, he would not be heard from again. He knew Herod's record of monstrous cruelty well enough to be certain of that.

Jesus suddenly and unexpectedly appeared right there in Jerusalem for the Passover ceremonies. He came to the temple and upset the regular routine of the observances by performing many miracles, signs and wonders there. As Nicodemus looked out on the courtyard and witnessed what Jesus was doing, his inquiring mind began searching for a way to be able to talk with Him privately.

There was a tremendous obstacle to doing that, however. Nicodemus was a member of the Sanhedrin, the highest council of the temple. This group of seventy elders was the "Supreme Court" of Judaism in all religious matters, and had taken an official position in opposition to Jesus and His ministry. They had condemned Him as an upstart religionist, radically liberal, who seemed to go out of His way to break the laws of the Sabbath. They also asserted that He associated with the wrong people and went to the wrong places according to their religious laws.

Should Nicodemus be seen talking to Jesus alone, he could then be accused of heresy and conspiracy against the Sanhedrin. Just associating with someone so irreligious was evidence enough to prosecute, judge and excommunicate even the highest ranking member.

But his desire to speak to Jesus privately was driving Nicodemus to the point where he was willing to take a dangerous risk. Only his wife knew what was tearing his soul apart, and she knew he was searching for that illusive answer to a question he had not as yet been able to verbalize. So one night, after the household was asleep, Nicodemus told his wife that he was going out to find Jesus. She assured him of her prayers for his safety, for by now she knew he could not be dissuaded from his search.

He stole silently out of the house and down the dark and narrow winding streets. Nicodemus ducked into the shadows of pillars and doorways whenever the moonlight threatened to make him visible to passing Roman sentries patrolling their assigned beats.

A Galilean like Jesus was most certainly not staying in the better part of the city with the orthodox Jews. So Nicodemus went southward across town to a lower part of the city where he knew he wouldn't be known, but where many devout followers of Jesus lived. The people were much poorer than those with whom Nicodemus normally socialized. In fact, when he had been down here before, it was only to pass through as quickly as possible.

Just over the south city wall and out far beyond was Gehenna, situated in the little valley of Hinnom. This was the site of the garbage dump where the waste of the temple's animal sacrifices was burned. Nicodemus could smell its stench by now. In one of Jesus' sermons, He had described the eternal destiny of the wicked as being like this dump (Matthew 5:30).

Suddenly two burly, boisterous men, each with a night woman on his arm, came down a side street toward him. Dare he ask them where he might find Jesus. What did he have to lose by asking? Being sure that they wouldn't know who he was, Nicodemus took a chance and inquired.

At first they taunted him for being dressed in such fine clothing. What was he doing down here alone in the middle of the night, anyway? It would have been easy for them to overcome him and rob him if they so chose. "Where is Jesus of Nazareth staying? Do you know?" Nicodemus begged.

"Why are you looking for Him? Do you want to turn Him over to the Sanhedrin, or do you plan to bust Him yourself?" growled the men as they grabbed Nicodemus by the collar of his fine robe, shaking their fists in his face.

"Would I come alone and ask you where He is if I wanted to do that?" he pleaded. "No, probably not," they responded, shoving him back. After he had straightened up his clothing, they told him that Jesus was staying at a house belonging to the family of one of his disciples, a young fellow named John. He lived a short distance up the street toward the temple in a better district. John's father was a wealthy fish merchant from Galilee who also had a house in Jerusalem. The two ruffians finally gave Nicodemus the directions, for everybody on this end of town knew where Jesus was staying. They knew He was the Friend of people like them.

Nicodemus walked the short distance quickly but quietly to the house of John's family. As he drew near, he saw that no lamps were burning. His heart was beating fast now as he gently rapped on the door. No response. He knocked louder. A man's startled voice responded, "Who's there? What do you want at this hour?" Nicodemus asked in a loud whisper, "Is Jesus of Nazareth staying here? Please let me talk to Him." The latch was unlocked and the door rattled open as the young man, big and brawny, opened the door and peered out into the dark. "Who are you?"

"My name is Nicodemus, and I'm alone. I've come to talk to Jesus for only a little while." The young man replied with impatient irritation, "Why can't you see Him at a decent hour tomorrow? He's sleeping now."

"But, I, I..." Nicodemus feared that though he was so close to his goal, he was yet so far away. Through an inner doorway, he saw that someone lit an oil lamp. Another man walked up behind the first and asked, "What's going on, John?" "It's all right, Master. It's just someone who wants to see You right now, but I'm getting rid of him."

"I think you can let him in, John. I'm awake now anyway." When John saw the fine clothing and the neatly trimmed beard, and when he heard the refined accent of Nicodemus, he argued that this stranger in the night with obvious authority couldn't be up to any good. But Jesus reassured him. "If it will make you feel any better," He said, "you can sit with us while we talk." John reluctantly allowed Nicodemus to enter. He indicated that they could go up on the flat roof of the house to talk. There they wouldn't disturb the sleep of anyone else. So these three dark figures silently climbed the stairs on the outside wall of the house up to the roof, where they sat down on two exterior support beams.

John sat silently, watching for any kind of a threatening move from Nicodemus. He quickly sensed the man's sincerity, however, and realized that he had taken a great risk doing what he was doing. John became sympathetic and began listening with interest. He didn't know that he was a witness to what became the most famous interview of all time, and it happened right there on his own roof top! (John 3:1-21)

When Nicodemus departed about an hour before dawn, his mind was ringing with such phrases as, "born again," "Holy Spirit," "God so loved the world," "eternal life," and "God didn't send His Son into the world to condemn the world, but to save it."

Was this the deep meaning of all those sacrifices he had offered in the temple for so many years? Is this why so many people were following Jesus wherever He proclaimed His message? He had known that God cared about His people, but weren't "His people" the Jews, those who were especially chosen through Abraham? What's this about God so loving the *world*? What kind of love was that? How could God love a person who was not a Jew?

Even though he was tired from his adventure all through the previous night, Nicodemus was not sleepy. As he performed his temple duties the following day, he couldn't dismiss these thoughts from his mind. One phrase really stood out—"born again." Was Jesus telling him that, even with his high rank in the religious system, he still might not see God in the end? Of all people—him?

We do not know whether, during the next two years, Nicodemus did anything more than seriously ponder what he had heard from Jesus. He may have come to a decision that he would not interfere with what Jesus was teaching, and he may have even come to accept Jesus for who He said He was—God's Son, the Messiah.

In any case, he chose to remain silent to everyone about the conclusion to which he had come. Considering his position on the Sanhedrin, his prestige in the temple, and his family's welfare, Nicodemus knew that all of this would be jeopardized if he ever revealed what he had heard from Jesus so secretly on that night-time pilgrimage.

But something happened that Nicodemus hadn't planned on. He knew the opposition to Jesus among his fellow religionists was growing more intense, and he had done his best to be a moderating influence on them (John 7:37-52).

He had almost been accused of being a sympathizer with Jesus, which would have brought the wrath of nearly all of the Sanhedrin down on his head. All he had done was suggest that they bring Jesus before them and let Him speak. Then they could ask Him questions. What's the harm in that? After all, it was not only fair and reasonable, but legal as well.

The majority of the members of the Sanhedrin had exploded, chiding this respected member as being sympathetic to the Galilean preacher. According to their Scriptures, no worthy prophet was ever supposed to come from Galilee. The meeting broke up in chaos.

Despite this humiliating episode, Nicodemus was not seriously questioned as to whether he was indeed sympathetic to the cause of Jesus of Nazareth. As far as the others knew, he was still uncommitted— and therefore safe.

We don't learn anything more about Nicodemus until perhaps a year or so later, though we do learn that there were other secret sympathizers with Jesus among the Jewish hierarchy. One of them was Joseph of Arimathaea. The Gospels of Mark and Luke tell us that he was also a member of the Sanhedrin, but that he had not consented with the majority in arresting Jesus.

It seems that the vote was by no means unanimous, and apparently Nicodemus was also a dissenter. But the reactionaries on the Sanhedrin carried the day and proceeded to petition the Roman Governor, Pontius Pilate, to crucify Jesus on the charge of insurrection against Rome. They knew that they could never have gotten Pilate's cooperation with a charge based only on religious blasphemy. Rome was not interested in their religion.

Jesus was crucified on a Friday. The Jewish Sabbath began at sundown and lasted until the same time on Saturday. It was not proper for any dead body to remain unburied over the Sabbath, so Joseph of Arimathaea went directly to Pilate and asked permission to remove Jesus' body from the cross and bury it. And, lo and behold, who should volunteer with him? Nicodemus! (John 19:38-42)

Not only did he assist in the removal of Jesus' body, but he brought about seventy-five pounds of myrrh and aloes as burial spices for embalming. Nicodemus didn't have to do that! There was no reason for a member of the Sanhedrin to lavish such attention on the body of this carpenter's son from Galilee. But such acts of quiet devotion could not be kept secret. His friend, Joseph, knew what Nicodemus meant by this gesture. So did the two women who witnessed the burial (Mark 15:47).

That secret and historic interview with Jesus Christ which happened more than two years before had come full circle in its prophetic impact. At that time, Jesus had also told Nicodemus, "Just as Moses lifted up the snake in the desert, so the Son of Man must be lifted up, that everyone who believes in Him may have eternal life" (John 3:14-15). From his accurate knowledge of the history of his nation Nicodemus knew what that meant:

Centuries before on their way to the Promised Land, as the people of Israel were slowly leaving Egypt behind by crossing the Sinai Peninsula, they became distressed and got angry at God and Moses for leading them into the barren desert. Poisonous snakes began to plague them and many died. The people interpreted this as a punishment for their complaining. So God told Moses to raise up an image of a serpent on a pole and all who looked upon it would be healed if they had been bitten (Numbers 21:4-9). (The symbol of one or two snakes entwined around a crossed pole is now the universal symbol of the medical profession, recognized around the world as representing the healing arts.)

That strange picture stuck in Nicodemus' mind all that time, but he knew not why. Then with the devastating impact of an earthquake, he suddenly realized what he was doing while helping Joseph lower the body of Jesus from off the pole upon which He had been lifted up! Now Nicodemus was up on that crossed pole *with* the body of Jesus, having been drawn to this time and place by an irresistible act through the providential leadership of God. Indeed he had been a teacher in Israel for so many years, but now at last he grasped the dynamic meaning of what Jesus had said, "So must the Son of Man be lifted up." And now Nicodemus had climbed up on that same cross with the Messiah from God!

+ + + + +

In every generation there have been secret believers in Jesus Christ The reasons are probably as many as these believers. You will not find any place in the Gospel where Jesus condemned anyone who chose to be an honest believer, and yet remain quiet about it, not wearing his faith on his sleeve like a military rank. In fact, Jesus commended the man who went into a closet to pray, but condemned the one who prayed on the street corner in pompous arrogance.

A genuine faith in Jesus Christ, while it may be quiet or even secret, has a way of eventually coming out in the open. It seems that there comes a time when there is no longer any resource of human origin to call upon for that indescribable spiritual energy to do the impossible, to bear the unbearable, to cross the uncrossable. It is then that trust in Christ, which is the available and ultimate spiritual bulwark for any who will believe in Him, cannot remain hidden any longer.

The problem with being a secret believer is that you are prevented from openly and freely lending that inner strength and spiritual resolve of Christ to a neighbor who may be inwardly crying for help. That neighbor may live next door or may go to your church; or maybe even lives in your own house. Faith may be quietly held in your heart, but the love it creates can't be bottled up. It will come out.

Chapter 6

A Woman
Caught in the Act

It was an open and shut case. There was no doubt that she was guilty.

The surest way to prove the guilt of someone accused of a crime is to present absolute and irrefutable evidence to a jury that the person was actually caught in the act of committing the crime. This is best done by offering witnesses—more than one—whose reputations for honesty cannot be questioned.

In New Testament times, about 1,850 years before photography was invented, eyewitnesses were relied upon to confirm who had committed a crime; the more eyewitnesses the better. With these, the conviction was certain.

On top of this, if there was already a specified punishment for that crime, then the doom of the criminal was also certain. And if the criminal was a woman in those days, then the eyewitness report of only two men was enough evidence to convict her.

Jesus was the center of a major controversy between most of the Jewish temple leaders and the huge number of followers who trusted Him. The temple leaders were desperate to find some way of trapping Him into saying something, doing something, or advocating something that would disgrace Him before all the people, or condemn Him before the Roman authorities. After all, Jesus' preaching was "rocking their religious boat" by upsetting the routine of ancient Judaism.

Suddenly they had the perfect setup to spring their trap. Somebody discovered an unnamed woman in bed with a man who was not her husband. The woman was reported as committing adultery, a capital offense.

Why was this crime regarded as so deadly serious? It was because when a man and a woman made their sacred vows before God to form a marriage, that relationship was intended to last as long as the both of them should live. The same vows today are just as sacred in the eyes of God. True, in those times, the marriage was often arranged by the couple's parents, who believed the bride's security and being a good mother for the children were essential elements.

Whether or not the couple loved each other was not the prime consideration in the relationship. This would grow with time, so they thought.

The people of Israel were taught that there was absolutely no excuse for a woman to commit adultery. The man was expected to be faithful too, though a man's sexual sins were more often overlooked, and sometimes even ignored.

Jesus taught that the man was equally responsible if he committed this sin. In the Sermon on the Mount, He placed the guilt equally on the man's shoulders, saying, "You have heard that it was said, 'Do not commit adultery.' But I tell you that anyone who looks at a woman lustfully has already committed adultery with her in his heart. If your right eye causes you to sin, gouge it out and throw it away. It is better for you to lose one part of your body than for your whole body to be thrown into hell" (Matthew 5:27-29).

The extreme condemnation that Jesus gave for the adulterous man is made even more graphic when one learns that the word translated as "hell" is the Greek word "gehenna." That was the name of the garbage dump just outside the south wall of Jerusalem where the entrails and other waste from the animal sacrifices from the temple were burned. If the wind blew just right, the stench was terrible. Essentially, Jesus taught that one who engaged in lust, let alone adultery, was lowering himself (and yes, herself) to the level of garbage!

+ + + + +

As Jesus was teaching the crowd in the temple courtyard, a group of pious, strict, temple leaders found this young woman, dragged her into the temple complex and dumped her right in front of Him.

The commotion caused the crowd to swell. The woman was half naked, scraped and bruised, disheveled and dirty. Her accusers had shown her no mercy, and they had long since learned that public humiliation was an excellent method of crime control, especially if it was done in broad daylight and among the worshipers in the temple.

No one seemed to have any interest in identifying the adulterous man, who was guilty of the same crime. Why was he not brought there, too? Was he the one who instigated the act? Would his position in society be ruined if his name was known? Would the woman's husband have tried to kill him? Or her? Was this adulterer a friend of her accusers, or maybe even one of them, desperately trying to cover his own guilt? That had happened before, and it certainly has been true in every generation since then.

Pointing their fingers at her, the accusers announced loudly enough for all to hear, "Teacher, this woman was caught in the act of adultery. In the Law Moses commanded us to stone such women" (Leviticus 20:10; Deuteronomy 22:20-24). "Now what do you say?" (John 8:4-5)

This question, particularly the way in which it had been presented in front of all these faithful temple worshipers, could have spelled disaster for Jesus and to the purpose for which He had come. To agree with them that she should be stoned to death would have gone against the law of the Romans. Only the Roman court, not the temple leaders, could pronounce a sentence of death by stoning.

On the other hand, if He chose to tell them to set her free, Jesus would be publicly taking a position against the law of Moses. This could mean being brought immediately before the Sanhedrin and being charged with advocating the breaking of the laws of the Old Testament, which were the foundation of the Jewish faith. Surely it appeared that He had no way to get out of this trap.

By this time, the poor, wretched young woman was crouched down on her knees, her clothing hanging on her in tatters. She trembled from fright, realizing that her life was in mortal danger no matter which answer Jesus gave. She bent over clear to the ground, covering her head with her hands as best she could. Her hair cascaded into the dust.

Amid scornful catcalls of the accusing men, with several angry women joining in, Jesus looked at the pitiful human castoff on the ground before Him. He said nothing. To the surprise of the onlookers around Him, including His fearful disciples, Jesus knelt down beside the terrified woman.

Those who believed that He was the Promised One from God, the Christ, the King of the Jews, gasped in disbelief as He lowered Himself down to the level of this guilt-ridden, shivering woman.

Still saying not a word, He placed one of His hands on her head over her two hands. Then with His other hand He began to write in the dirt upon which they were both kneeling: "Idolater, profane, irreverent, disrespectful of God, disrespectful of family, murderer, adulterer, thief, liar, lustful, covetous." (See the Ten Commandments, Exodus 20:1-17.)

The author of this account does not tell us what Jesus actually wrote in the dirt, which is the only record we have of Jesus writing anything. He may have written words which describe the breaking of the Ten Commandments. His implication was that if these accusers were going to invoke the authority of the laws given to Moses, they had better first see if there were any which they themselves had broken. If so, were they prepared to stone each other? The fact that they were accusing a woman made no difference at all to Jesus.

One by one, the accusers looked down to see what Jesus was writing. Loudly they continued to demand His answer, still not seeing the point that He was making. They did not realize that He was about to cast an arrow into the heart of each of them.

Jesus stood up for a moment, looked at each of them squarely in the eye and shouted, "All right, hurl the stones at her until she dies." The startled girl on the ground shrieked, "No! No!" Her heart jumped in terror. But Jesus hadn't finished yet. "If any one of you is without sin, let him be the first to throw a stone at her" (John 8:7).

He knelt down beside her again, as if He was willing to take her punishment along with her. He wrote in the dust once more. He had met these accusers before and knew their hearts. He scratched each of their names beside the sin they themselves had committed.

Again, the accusers saw the words Jesus was writing, but now their meaning could not have been clearer. Beginning with the oldest among them, each of the woman's accusers turned and silently cowered away from the crowd in shame and embarrassment. Many of the onlookers saw them for what they really were—frauds! Hypocrites!

The courtyard was silent and tense as the remaining people waited to see what Jesus would do next. Slowly He rose again and looked around. The taunting mob was gone. He reached down, took one of her hands still covering her head, and lifted the trembling soul to her feet as she clung to the shredded garment about her waist.

Jesus never did ask her if she was guilty of the sin of adultery. She knew it and so did He—and so did all the onlookers. Instead, He asked her "Woman, where are they? Has no one condemned you?" In frightened, sobbing tones, she replied, "No one, Sir." Then Jesus said to her ever so gently, "Then neither do I condemn you...Go now and leave your life of sin" (John 8:10-11).

Just then a breeze came up and blew away the words written in the dust.

The people stood amazed and transfixed at what they had just witnessed. Never had they seen such love and forgiveness quite like this shown by any priest or rabbi, or even another person. Tears streamed down the faces of both women and men in the crowd, for they knew they had just seen the love of God made known clearly.

Still weeping, an older, gray-haired lady stepped forward out of the group, removed the shawl from her head and shoulders and wrapped it comfortingly around this forgiven girl. "Come to my house with me, and I'll help you recover, my dear." The two walked away arm in arm. This kind of love is contagious. Jesus watched them leave—and smiled.

+ + + + +

It is the Lord of Heaven and earth who was willing to assume the place of punishment for our sins, to become as if guilty in our place. This was the whole point of the life of Christ. And His death on the Cross, His burial, and most of all His glorious resurrection achieved all that.

The divine love of a merciful God is not demonstrated in shouts of condemnation, by a waving, clenched fist, or by pointing an accusing finger.

Yes, sin brings guilt and guilt brings punishment. The law of Moses shows us that sin is the transgression of God's laws, which were established for the benefit and preservation of the human race. The breaking of these laws will eventually cause humanity to be annihilated from the face of the earth.

The only way that God could preserve His creation was to forgive the sin, remove the guilt, take away the punishment, and bring about a change of heart in every individual who will accept this new birth of spirit. This is what Jesus the Christ brings to us all.

Chapter 7

John:
A Spoiled Brat

It took him a long time to make it from "brat" to "beloved," but he made it.

How frequently do we read a comparison of the mature, fulfilled individual with what appeared to be the opposite sort of person, or nearly so, in his or her younger days. Once they have made their mark on the world scene, it is often hard to imagine that in their younger days some people were very different.

One would be amazed at the contrast, even to the point of wondering if the biographer got two separate individuals mixed up. Some of history's most outstanding leaders began their lives in deplorable circumstances; yet they developed into positions of leadership, power and sometimes wealth, which bore little if any resemblance to their youth.

Just as astounding are the stories of some who were responsible, devout and accomplished as youths, and were reared in favorable circumstances. Yet because of some crisis created either by themselves or others, they turned out to be human shipwrecks on history's rocky shores.

It is this fascination we have in studying human beings that causes us to never lose interest in ourselves. When all is said and done, there is no way to accurately predict how a person is going to turn out, in spite of what some astrologers might say.

Such a man was the disciple of Jesus named John (not to be confused with John the Baptist). He is a classic study in contrasts—the "before and after" of a new creation in Christ Jesus.

The influence of John the Baptist reached far beyond his place of ministry at the south end of the Jordan River. Andrew, the brother of Simon Peter, had heard John the Baptist preach and became a follower of him for a time. He heard the Baptist's mighty declaration of Jesus as the Lamb of God (John 1:35-37). He then did as the Baptizer had instructed him and others to do: He began to follow Jesus.

When Andrew went north to Galilee, he found his brother, Simon Peter, and introduced him to Jesus.

Jesus called them both to come and follow Him to become "fishers of men."

These two brothers apparently worked in a thriving fishing business with another pair of brothers, James and John, the sons of Zebedee (Luke 5:10). Considering the heavy diet of fish at that time in Israel, we would be mistaken to think that these were "poor" fishermen. Not so, for when Jesus called James and John to follow Him, they left their father and the "hired servants." The only people who employed hired servants were those with money. These were not slaves, but servants who worked for a wage or for a share in the profits of the business (Mark 1:20).

Though James and John worked with their father, the personalities of these two boys indicate that they were both self-indulgent, pampered and spoiled. It would seem that Jesus would have wanted to pick someone who did not need so much reforming in order to change them into the useful apostles they needed to become. But as the end results proved, He knew what He was doing. This young man named John became known to the Christian world from his day to ours as the "Apostle of Love" and is a lasting testimony to Christ's transforming power.

The story of John begins when Jesus called him and his brother James to follow Him and become fishermen of people. There seems to have been no protest on their father's part and no effort to try to hold them back from Jesus' call. We might speculate that he felt it was best for these boys to get away from home and learn to become responsible men. Or maybe he felt they needed to get away from their doting mother. Perhaps he just wanted them to "get out of his hair" with their constant demands for privileges of which they were not yet worthy.

In any case, they followed Jesus without hesitation. From the great prologue, or introduction to John's own Gospel (John 1:1-18), which he wrote more than half a century later, it is easy to see the great influence John the Baptist had on this younger John. Whether he met the Baptist before he began following Jesus or later, or at all, we don't know. But the burning passion of the Baptist's message as to who Jesus was began the long process of young John's transformation.

Every young person must have ambitions, goals and desires if he or she is to amount to anything worthwhile in life. Sometimes young people are misdirected by others, or they aim in the wrong direction, or too high, or too low. But most want to rise out of the ordinary and commonplace and be unique, different, better or even the best at something.

John certainly did not have it in mind to be a fisherman his entire life. He may have been good at that occupation, but his eye was set on other goals. Little wonder that some of Jesus' disciples had nicknames (i.e. Peter the Rock, Simon the Zealot). But Jesus called James and John "the Sons of Thunder" (Mark 3:17).

It is easy to see why He dubbed them so. In the earlier years, we see these young brothers complaining about those to whom Jesus ministered. We see them attempting to bring vengeance on people and trying to trample over the other disciples in gaining positions above them. They were acting like a couple of "brats." The virtual absence of any spirit of love during these formative years is apparent. How, indeed, could Jesus have picked these two without soon realizing the headaches that were to come with them?

While on a journey from Galilee, Jesus asked some of His disciples to go to a certain village in Samaria to reserve some overnight accommodations. However, because of intense racial hatred on both sides, any Jew traveling through Samaria was not welcomed to stay there over night. Jesus had encountered such an experience earlier when He met the Samaritan woman at Jacob's well (John 4).

The disciples were turned down flat. James and John exploded at this insult by these "half-breed dogs." Seething with anger, these "Sons of Thunder" demanded of Jesus, "Lord, do You want us to call fire down from heaven and destroy them? But He turned and rebuked them." (Some other biblical manuscripts add, "And He said, 'You do not know what kind of spirit you are of, for the Son of Man did not come to destroy men's lives, but to save them' ") (Luke 9:54-56).

Can the same young man who was so angered by racial prejudice, and who immediately wanted to burn up his enemies to get revenge for an insult be the same man who is later known as the Apostle of Love? Certainly he showed no love here.

The mother of James and John had been the principal influence in shaping the obnoxious attitude of these boys. We aren't told her name, but she may have been the woman named Salome mentioned in Mark 15:40. If only one of these brothers had exhibited such an attitude, then we might be wrong to assume that their mother was such a problem, for some good would have come from her to the other son. But when both were alike in this respect, and when we read that their father by all appearances was a responsible and prosperous provider, we are left with little choice than to assume that Mamma was the source of their bad dispositions.

Rather than training them to realize that they must earn the right to be leaders among people, she sought special privileges and positions for them. This event happened near the end of Jesus' ministry, after John and the other disciples had been with Him for about three years. They were walking from the Jordan River toward Jerusalem (as it turned out for the last time), and the crowds that followed earlier had gone home now. They were all alone, except that James' and John's mother was with them (Matthew 20:17-24; Mark 10:35-45).

Jesus knew what awaited Him in Jerusalem, and He described it to His disciples: "We are going up to Jerusalem, and the Son of Man will be betrayed to the chief priests and the teachers of the law. They will condemn Him to death and will turn Him over to the Gentiles to be mocked and flogged and crucified. On the third day He will be raised to life!" (Matthew 20:17-19)

Prior to this prediction of catastrophe, Jesus had talked about the blessings of the Kingdom of Heaven which is of course what the disciples preferred to hear. The significance of Jesus' prophecy apparently didn't register in their thinking; certainly not in the minds of these "Sons of Thunder" or their mother.

She stepped forward just then, bringing her two sons with her, and promptly asked Jesus for a favor. She was not concerned as to whether they were worthy of any favors or not; her intention was that they should receive them regardless of their being worthy.

"What is it you want?" Jesus asked. She replied, "Grant that one of these two sons of mine may sit at Your right and the other at Your left in Your kingdom."

But Jesus, astounded at the audacity of her request, replied, "You don't know what you are asking..."

He then turned to James and John and asked them, "Can you drink the cup I am going to drink?" (Matthew 20:20-22)

"Yes," they responded flippantly, "we are able!" "You shall indeed drink from it," He told them. "But I have no right to say who will sit on the thrones next to Mine. Those places are reserved for the persons My Father selects." The Gospel of Mark refers to the same incident, except the mother is not mentioned as a party to the request of James and John.

When the other disciples discovered what James and John had asked for, they were understandably indignant. So Jesus called all of them together and said, "You know that those who are regarded as rulers of the Gentiles lord it over them, and their high officials exercise authority over them. Not so with you. Instead, whoever wants to become great among you must be your servant, and whoever wants to be first must be slave of all. For even the Son of Man did not come to be served, but to serve, and to give His life as a ransom for many" (Mark 10:41-45).

In those days, being a servant to someone for a short while meant that one would receive either pay or a reward of some kind. But to be a slave at all would certainly be beneath the status of any of Zebedee's family.

The words that Jesus said to James and John and their mother must have sunk into their hearts profoundly, especially the mother. Matthew refers to her again at the time of Jesus' crucifixion: "Many women were there, watching from a distance. They had followed Jesus from Galilee to care for His needs. Among them were Mary Magdalene, Mary the mother of James and Joses, and the mother of Zebedee's sons" (Matthew 27:55-56). Apparently she learned the lesson of what it meant to serve and the high cost of serving Jesus Christ.

For the entire time that James and John were with Jesus, the other disciples had tolerated their arrogant, abrasive attitudes, but not without some dissension. The other disciples trusted them the least of all among their group, especially after their request for special positions in Jesus' kingdom, which they still thought He was going to set up politically.

By contrast, Judas Iscariot the treasurer of the group, was considered the most trustworthy of all of the disciples.

A life-changing crisis had to come, and it came at the Last Supper. We can understand the impact of Jesus' final week on John when we realize that almost half of his Gospel is a detailed description of Jesus' teaching and actions during that one week alone.

Considering what John had been like up to that time, it seems incredible that in his Gospel he identifies himself several times, not by his name or the pronoun "I," but as "the disciple whom Jesus loved." It's not hard to understand this, however, if we realize that Jesus may have been the *only* one in the group who really did love John, as selfish, ambitious, temperamental, intolerant and childish a brat as he had been. Jesus has always loved the people who were the hardest for humanity to love in order to show us how truly deep is God's love.

We may wonder why Jesus chose Peter, James and John as His "inner circle" of disciples. Why were they on the Mount of Transfiguration with Him (Luke 9:28-36)? Later, why were they separated from the others and led by Jesus a little further into the garden of Gethsemane to pray (Mark 14:32-34)?

Perhaps it was because Jesus knew that the heaviest responsibilities for the yet-to-be-born Church would fall upon these three in its formative years. Maybe Jesus realized that they were starting farther back than the others. They had much more to learn and would have a harder time learning it. Perhaps to Jesus, they were "diamonds in the rough," uncut, unpolished and without a proper setting. It would take more effort, patience and perseverance to make them into qualified leaders for the Church, which was about to change the course of history. No wonder only John records Jesus' prayer in Gethsemane for His disciples (John 17). He was there when Jesus prayed it!

During the Last Supper in the quiet upper room in Jerusalem, Jesus shocked His disciples by announcing that one of them would betray Him to those who sought to silence Him. They began to question each other as to who would ever do such a thing, and then they broke into an argument about who among them was the greatest. You can be sure that John was in the middle of that one (Luke 22:21-27).

Jesus repeated again the lesson they had had such a hard time learning, that in His Kingdom, a leader must be a servant of all. Surely if Jesus' body was to be crucified on the cross, His heart must have been crucified at that table that night.

John tells about his own experience at that moment with a poignancy that could only be felt by one who was finally realizing the truth about himself. "One of them, the disciple whom Jesus loved, was reclining next to Him. Simon Peter motioned to this disciple, 'Ask Him which one He means' " (John 13:23-24).

John might have sprung back at Peter saying something like, "Why ask me? How am I supposed to know a thing like that?" Did Peter suspect John, sitting there so close to Jesus, but perhaps with deceit in his heart? If Jesus was foretelling a future unplanned betrayal to be carried out by someone who would never have dreamed he could do such a thing, then was He possibly talking about John? He knew that the men sitting around that table wouldn't put it past him.

But repeating the setting again, he writes, "Leaning back against Jesus, he asked Him, 'Lord, who is it?' " (John 13:25) Jesus revealed to the other disciples that the betrayer was to be Judas. Judas? Impossible! Not him! Loyal, trusted, faithful, prudent Judas! No one else knew why Jesus talked to Judas just then. The most likely prospect for such an act was still John. And now he realized it himself. That was the last argument between the disciples over betrayal or greatness.

Later that night, after Jesus had been arrested and taken to the court of the high priest, John entered the court along with Jesus, but Peter stayed outside. John went back to get Peter to bring him in, but it was at that time that Peter was accused by those in the courtyard of being a friend of Jesus. He denied it three times before the rooster crowed early that morning, as Jesus had predicted to Peter himself.

John witnessed this tragic triple denial and realized how he was the one most suspected of being capable of what Judas and Peter had actually done. Then he saw himself as the other disciples had seen him during the past three years: untrustworthy, scheming, conniving, even capable of betraying their Master if that's what it took to climb to the top of what he conceived to be a Jewish political kingdom.

John: A Spoiled Brat

The full impact of the change Jesus made in John's life came on the following day when Jesus was hanging on the cross. In His dying moments, Jesus spoke to both His mother, Mary, and to John, who was standing next to her at the foot of the cross. Jesus called to Mary amid His excruciating pain, "Woman, behold your son." No, He was not telling her to look upon Him hanging on that cross. Instead, He was saying to her, "Woman, behold your new son, John, who needs you now." Then He looked down upon John, who was realizing that all of his self-centered ambitions and future plans were being crucified on that cross with his Lord. The dreams of greatness he had harbored were being splattered on the ground with the shed blood from that cross.

Jesus said to John, "Behold, your mother." Why would He say that? Jesus knew how unlovable and obnoxious John had been. But He also knew that he was a young man truly capable of teaching many generations what was involved in the deepest meaning of love. And who could teach that to John any better than Mary, the mother of Christ, the Son of God.

Where his own mother had such a shallow, selfish, scheming attitude regarding the future of her sons, now John was facing the responsibility for caring for the one woman in all the world who knew more about the joy and the pain involved in true love than any other human being. And she came to live in John's own home in Jerusalem from that hour.

We can no more leave this biography of John the Beloved with him walking away from the foot of the cross than we can leave the life of Jesus with Him still hanging on the cross. Neither story ended there.

After Jesus' body was taken down from the cross and placed in the tomb belonging to Joseph of Arimathaea, black clouds of despondency overcame the disciples and followers of their slain Leader.

John, along with Jesus' mother and the other disciples, were gathered together in a house in Jerusalem. Early in the morning, however, Mary Magdalene and two other women decided to take a walk out to the cemetery just beyond the city wall to place some embalming spices in the tomb.

Sunday morning, Mary Magdalene and the others with her walked to the tomb where Jesus had been buried—and found it empty! The body which had been placed there the previous Friday evening had been stolen. Why couldn't Pilate, the Governor of Judea, have prevented this sacrilege?

Mary Magdalene was startled beyond words when she turned around and saw a man standing beside her. She couldn't see him clearly through her tears. Assuming he was only the gardener, she asked him, "If you have taken Him somewhere, please tell me?" Then came the voice she knew so well. He spoke her name, "Mary." John, himself, is the one who recorded this incident. The stunned woman raced into Jerusalem and became the first person in history to announce that Jesus Christ had risen from the dead. Peter, the big, burly fisherman and John the disciple whom only Jesus loved ran immediately to the tomb. There, two messengers of God met them and confirmed what Mary had declared. He was risen back to life again!

John records that a few days later, Jesus and His disciples were gathered on the shore of Lake Galilee, where they had started their three-year adventure together. It was now time for Jesus to depart from them. But first He gave instructions to Peter. He asked him if he now understood the real meaning of love for Christ and for the "sheep" of the yet-to-be-born Church. Peter thought he understood, but when Jesus pressed the issue, Peter soon got irritated, which was not unusual for him. (Compare Peter's response to St. Paul's definition of love in First Corinthians 13:5.)

Jesus gave Peter a verbal picture of Peter's own life by saying that one day he would be compelled to go where he would not want to go in order to fulfill Christ's call. Apparently John overheard this conversation.

One may doubt that Peter really comprehended at that time what self-sacrificing love meant. He abruptly cut off Jesus and pointed at John, who was standing nearby listening. He then asked Jesus, "And Lord, what shall this man do?"

Jesus answered Peter, "If I want him to live until I come again, that is none of your business, Peter.

You must make sure you follow Me where I lead you." It was evident that Peter still doubted the change in John even after the resurrection of Jesus (John 21:20-24).

The jealousy of all the disciples once again surfaced against John. They thought Jesus had told him he would not die, which of course, is not at all what He said.

For the disciples to believe that John could have changed so radically from what he used to be was apparently more than their hearts and minds could accept. From the uttermost to the uttermost—that was the story of John the "brat" becoming John the Beloved.

+ + + + +

James, the brother of John, became the first of the disciples of Jesus martyred. He was put to death by King Herod Agrippa I around 44 A.D. His fervid preaching caused the Jewish enemies of Christianity to hate him, and they were glad when his mouth was silenced by the king.

How accurate was the prophecy of the Lord when He said that James should "drink of the same cup" from which He was to drink.

John the Beloved, who became the exact opposite of the brat he had been during his younger years, served as an apostle in the early Church, primarily in Ephesus. This city was as pagan as any place in the world at that time. Serving as the Christian leader of that new church tested the limits of John's love for the idol-worshiping people of that city.

Though Paul founded the church in Ephesus, John became its pastor. It was probably from there that John wrote his Gospel and the three short letters that bear his name in the New Testament. Each of these writings emphasizes the forgiving nature of the love which he called "agape." This is the love that Christ Jesus demonstrated to an undeserving world when He died on the cross for all our sin.

One of John's purposes in writing these manuscripts was to combat a heresy called gnosticism. This teaching held that Christ was only a phantom or a ghost, sent by God into the world. He was therefore not really dead before He came out of the tomb as the risen Lord. John clashes with this false teaching and defeats it in his Gospel, Chapters 1:1-18 and 21:24-25, and also in Second John 6-7.

In the Book of Revelation, which John wrote while in forced exile on Patmos, a small island off the west coast of Turkey, he wrote to the churches of Asia Minor among which he had worked for many years. At the time he wrote it he was probably over the age of 90. He wrote of judgment and of joy, of faith and the future, but he especially wrote of love and liberty (Revelation 2:1-7). In this book he recorded these tender words of Jesus, "Here I am! I stand at the door and knock. If anyone hears My voice and opens the door, I will come in and eat with him, and he with me" (Revelation 3:20).

What a far cry this is from the old attitude of the young John, who was willing to call down fire upon anyone he didn't like. Jesus Christ made the difference. And His transforming power is still the same for anyone who will believe on Him as the risen Son of God.

Chapter 8

Martha, Mary and Lazarus: A Close-Knit Family

The excitement of life is seldom found in one's daily routine, unless something happens to make that routine seem like a monumental achievement. For some, the excitement comes when the daily grind is broken and replaced with something or someone who captures their undivided attention and makes them forget the chores for a while.

In the 20th Century, there are so many things that can divert our attention away from the daily routine that it has become rather uncommon to find someone so locked into their rigid schedule that they are made irritable or insecure if their regimen is upset.

It was an effort to make the routine of preparing meals and doing dishes a more spiritually rewarding experience, when one housewife hung a plaque over her kitchen sink that said, "This is my daily prayer chapel." However, she didn't always find it so, but it helped.

Martha was the elder sister in this family of two sisters and a brother. Jesus had known Martha, Mary and Lazarus for some time. We don't know when or where they met, but it was probably when Jesus was passing through Bethany, their home town not far from Jerusalem.

It appears that none of these three had ever been married. They were probably in their 30's or older at the time we first read about them in Luke 10:38-42. We can assume that their parents were dead, probably leaving a substantial inheritance to them. They had decided that they would not break up their relationship, but instead continued to live together in the family home. Luke doesn't mention Lazarus, but John's Gospel focuses on a major miracle of Jesus' divine power (John 11 and 12).

On one occasion, Jesus and His disciples were walking through Bethany when Martha invited Him to stay for dinner at their home. There is no mention of His companions staying there with Him, for only Jesus, Martha and Mary seemed to be involved in this incident. Even Lazarus, who we learn from John's Gospel was well known among the Jewish leaders in both Bethany and Jerusalem, was probably not at home when Jesus arrived. If Jesus' disciples were expected for dinner, then we can sympathize all the more with Martha's dilemma.

As Martha was preparing dinner for her special Guest, Mary became so intrigued with what Jesus was saying that she stopped helping Martha, leaving the entire task to her sister alone. We aren't told what fascinating subject was being discussed.

We do know from the comments of others that Jesus was extremely gifted both as a public speaker and a personal conversationalist. We therefore need not be surprised that Mary became captivated by His words to the point where she was sitting before Him on the floor in rapt attention, forgetting her duties in the kitchen.

But Martha—practical, industrious, busy Martha—was not so captivated by Jesus' words. In fact, she was irritated that her Guest would allow her to bear the work of preparing dinner alone, while Mary irresponsibly neglected her share. Apparently Martha decided that the best tact would be to have Jesus tell Mary, "You had best go help your sister now, and we will talk about this later." This, she thought, would not insult Jesus for failing to recognize her frustration. He could then resume His conversation at the table or after dinner, and include both Martha and Mary.

But Martha received a most unexpected surprise when Jesus complimented her on her efficiency as a homemaker and as a hostess, but then added that Mary preferred to listen to Him, and that she should remain with Him while Martha went ahead and finished her work.

Luke was decent enough not to record Martha's response to this rebuff, but it isn't likely that she returned to her task very satisfied with Jesus' answer. It seems that often a friendship doesn't become truly firm and close until the people involved find the outer limits of each other's tolerance and patience.

Martha found out what both her sister and Jesus considered to be most important to them. And Jesus and Mary both discovered what was most critical to this fine hostess, Martha. Considering the fact that the Bible shows that their close relationship continued, they did not allow their friendship to fall apart over this incident, which certainly could have left scars on the souls of each of them.

Martha could easily have become deeply angry at Jesus for being a "typical male" of that day. She could have been jealous toward Mary for capturing the attention of Jesus, even to the point where He was more concerned with continuing His conversation with Mary than in eating the meal which Martha was diligently preparing for Him. After all, wasn't Martha the one who invited Him for dinner?

To overcome her impatience with Mary and her emotional conflict with Jesus makes Martha the heroine of this incident, which was a small crisis brought on by Jesus Himself.

+ + + + +

John brings us the record of another crisis in the life of this family and their friend, Jesus, that was anything but small (John 11:1-26—12:11).

To put this story in proper perspective, we need to understand that Matthew, Mark and Luke regarded the amazing, supernatural acts of Jesus as "miracles." They always report them as positive indications that Jesus was indeed more than ordinary humanity. He is clearly beyond the status of being a mere magician on the basis of two qualities: first, that each of the miracles was performed in order to help somebody where there was no other help available; and second, they were performed in order to make a critical point in a lesson that Jesus was attempting to make clear to His listeners.

Many of the miracles Jesus performed involved altering the normal course of nature or meeting an immediate need. John, in his Gospel, develops a progression of Jesus' miracles beginning with His turning water into wine (Chapter 2), and increasing in significance up to this event involving Lazarus. John writes as if he wants us to climb a stairway of faith in coming to our understanding of who Jesus really was and is.

As John reflected back years later over the days when Jesus walked the earth with him, he had time to think about what those miracles really meant. They were not intended solely to do good for people or to display Jesus' power and convince people to listen to His message. Beyond all of that, John understood that Jesus was able to alter nature because He was One with God the Creator.

John was able to discern in these miracles their true and complete meaning: that Jesus came to this earth as the God-Man enwrapped in one Person. The miracles He performed were "signs" pointing to His true and complete identity, even as a road sign points to a destination.

Matthew's Gospel identifies Jesus as the King of the Jews, the Messiah. Mark shows Him as the suffering Servant of God and man. Luke points toward Jesus as the Savior of the world. But each of these portrayals is in a *horizontal* relationship to the human race.

John, on the other hand, aims to present Jesus, step by miraculous step, as the only begotten Son of God with all divine power and forgiving grace for every person who will receive Him as Savior and Lord. This is the unique *vertical* relationship of Jesus with God the Father, which is not parallel to the structure of the other three Gospel records.

The event involving Lazarus was the "point on the pyramid" of the signs and wonders Jesus did which affected people other than Himself. Jesus and His companions were away from Jerusalem because of the opposition against Him. His life could be in serious danger from the hierarchy of the temple who saw Jesus as a threat to their established religious order. The crowds following Jesus were immense to say the least. No one had attracted throngs of people like this since the days of John the Baptist.

Jesus, therefore, had gone with His companions to the wilderness to the east on the opposite side of the Jordan River. This was not far from the hometown of Judas Iscariot. While Jesus was there, Lazarus became gravely ill, and Martha and Mary feared for his life. As far as they were concerned, the only One who could heal him was Jesus. They knew that He had healed many people who He didn't even know—how much more would He want to help Lazarus, who was a close friend.

It is significant that when these sisters sent someone to tell Jesus about Lazarus' illness and to urge Him to come quickly, they apparently knew exactly where He could be found. Because of the danger to Jesus' life, His whereabouts was unknown to the temple leaders. This indicates that these three were close, trusted friends.

While Jesus was there in the wilderness, many who had heard the preaching of John the Baptist came to hear this One whom the Baptizer had introduced three years before at the baptism of Jesus in the Jordan River.

The messengers from Mary and Martha found Jesus quickly and relayed the news about Lazarus. They wanted Jesus to discontinue His preaching immediately and come with them to heal Lazarus before he died. Even though Jesus loved that family intensely, He chose to remain where He was for two more days.

Apparently the earlier incident when Jesus had rebuffed Martha continued to be an irritation to her. As far as she was concerned, this delay was threatening the life of her beloved brother. Didn't the messengers make clear the urgency of the situation? Surely Jesus would not play games with her and Mary at a time like this. How could He be so unfeeling and callous toward them in an emergency like this?

The decision was not that simple, however. The disciples argued with Jesus, probably for those entire two days, about even going near Jerusalem again, for they knew that there was bound to be an attempt to take His life. It had been tried the last time He was there. Those disciples were not interested in imperiling their own lives either. We can be sure that Jesus listened to their pleadings.

A decision had to be made, however, and Jesus finally made it. He was going to Lazarus. He told His companions, "Our friend Lazarus is sleeping." They responded, "Well, Lord, if he is sleeping, that's good. Perhaps he will soon recover." But then Jesus told them plainly from His own inner revelation, "Lazarus is dead!"

They each felt a sense of sorrowful relief when they learned that the life struggle of Lazarus was over. To the disciples, this meant that now there was no need to hurry. Perhaps they could go to Mary and Martha when at least some of the danger at Jerusalem had subsided. But again Jesus showed His contrary nature to "normal" logic and announced, "Let's go to him now!"

Thomas, the doubting disciple who had yet to make his mark on history and who seemed to be the chronic pessimist among them, shrugged his shoulders and declared that they all might as well go and die with Jesus. He saw no hope for the future if they encountered the temple leaders again, which was almost sure to happen since Bethany was so close to Jerusalem. The news that Jesus was coming always seemed to be announced well ahead of His arrival.

By the time Jesus got to Bethany, Lazarus had been dead for four days and his body had already begun to decompose. As soon as Martha heard that Jesus had arrived, she went out to meet Him, possibly at the cemetery where He had come to join the mourners.

Martha, with understandably passionate feeling, said, "Lord, if You had only come right away, my brother wouldn't have died. You could have prevented this. You could have healed him as You have done with so many others." Once again she poured out her frustration at what she saw as Jesus' response to her wishes.

It was not the common practice of that day for a woman in Israel to receive a formal religious education. But the conversation that followed indicates that Martha and Mary had either learned much from their brother, Lazarus, or from his Pharisee friends, or from Jesus Himself as He taught them about God's promise of a resurrection to new life.

When Jesus told her, "Your brother will rise again," Martha didn't seem surprised at His statement. She responded, "I know that he will rise again in the resurrection at the last day." But Jesus didn't stop with that statement. He went on to the very core of her faith. "I am the resurrection and the life. He who believes in Me will live, even though he dies; and whoever lives and believes in Me will never die. Do you believe this?" (John 11:25-26)

Martha could not comprehend the full meaning of Jesus' declaration. Nor could she have gained an understanding of what Jesus was about to do just from His words alone. It is not required that one have a complete revelation of all that our faith in Christ provides. Martha simply answered Jesus from her heart, "Yes, Lord; I believe that You are the Christ, the Son of God, He who is coming into the world."

John records her answer in words that are remarkably like his own in the first chapter of his Gospel.

Whether Martha fully understood what Jesus taught her about a faith which reaches beyond obvious reality, and even beyond human imagination, we cannot be sure.

Martha then called her sister, Mary, who had remained at home. Several of the Jewish leaders with whom Lazarus had been associated for so many years were with her to comfort and console her.

When Martha told her that Jesus was at the cemetery and wanted to see her, she jumped up as if the only One that mattered had finally arrived. To the surprise of all their guests, both women rushed out of the house. Their friends followed them, not knowing what to expect next.

When Mary ran to Jesus, she fell on her knees, sobbing in deep grief. "Lord, if You had been here, my brother would not have died." Jesus was moved to tears. As Mary, Martha and their many friends gathered about, some of the Jews remarked, "If this man opened the eyes of the blind man, couldn't He have kept Lazarus from dying?" Certainly none of them, in their wildest imagination, could have dreamed what Jesus was about to do.

Jesus wept at the loss of Lazarus with as genuine a grief as even his sisters. It may well have been that He had not even thought about doing any wondrous "sign" or miracle until that moment, and was accepting Lazarus' death as He would that of any other human friend.

This situation was certainly assembled by the Spirit of God, perhaps even as the occasion where Jesus turned the water into wine at the wedding feast three years before. No one was asking Him now to raise Lazarus back to life then and there, for none of them would have expected to see such a thing happen in their lifetime.

John repeated his exclamation that Jesus was deeply moved. We can only imagine how strong each of those emotions were, but they were not the same. The first was human grief; the second was due to the surge of divine power that was filling His soul. Even then, Jesus had to ask where the grave of Lazarus was located—a very human inquiry.

Lazarus, having been dead four days and already decomposing, was in no condition to have the huge stone removed that covered his burial cave. But Jesus called for the stone to be removed anyway. Martha, always the practical one, told Jesus that there would be a putrid smell in there, supposing that Jesus was going to enter the tomb. Not so.

Jesus, no longer weeping, but with majestic, divine strength in His voice, replied to her, "Did not I tell you that if you believe you would see the glory of God?" Martha stood speechless, as did Mary and all the others.

Then Jesus prayed loudly enough for all to plainly hear, "Father, I thank Thee that Thou hast heard Me..." Jesus wished so deeply that Lazarus would return that His wish became the ultimate prayer of faith, and the ultimate testimony of Him as the Son of God.

Lifting His arms toward the open tomb, Jesus shouted at the top of His voice, "Lazarus, come forth!" The crowd around the tomb gasped, stunned in total amazement as they saw the body laying inside begin to move. Wrapped in a burial shroud, it gradually sat up on the stone slab, then slowly stood. Lazarus walked out of that stench-laden cave, leaving death and decay behind. Jesus ordered those standing by to unwrap Lazarus from his burial shroud and let him go.

To have made this happen, Jesus had to *re-create* living flesh and blood into the body of this man who was dead, through His power as One with the Creator of all life.

For any among that crowd to have doubted, they would have had to deny what they actually saw and heard that day. The only other choice was to admit the obvious: Jesus was indeed the Son of God.

This was the greatest "sign" that John recorded in identifying who Jesus truly was. But more than that, John also indicated that the resurrection of Lazarus was a prophetic sign pointing to the fact that Jesus would Himself be raised from the dead after His own death on the cross.

Lazarus was raised by a power *outside* Himself, but later died a second time. Jesus was raised to life by a divine power of God, which left His body temporarily in death, but returned it to new life in a resurrected body, composed of a substance not limited to the confines of walls or space or time.

Such is the promise of eternal life to every believer. John recorded this astounding event to assure those of us who believe in Jesus Christ of the certain hope we have in the final resurrection. If the doubter wishes to reject that eternal hope, what other hope is there?

Real Discoveries

Questions for Study and Discussion

Suggestion for group study: Assign one question to each student who will study the question and report the results at the next meeting. Reports should be limited to five minutes each, with no interruptions. Listeners should make notes as the material is being presented. After all reports have been given on the entire chapter, *then* open the meeting for discussion.

Chapter 1— Joseph: A Common Man

A. Should God warn and prepare a person for a crisis that is soon to come? Was He fair in telling Mary, but not Joseph, of their impending crisis? Is God always fair?

B. If Joseph blamed God for the moral dilemma that Mary found herself in, did he commit a sin? Explain.

C. What do Joseph's encounters with God's angel tell us about the faith of this common, ordinary man?

D. Joseph was considered a "righteous" man. Explain what you think this means. What qualities equipped Joseph to be the appointed father for Jesus, God's Son?

Chapter 2—Mary: A Mother of an Uncommon Son

A. It is obvious that Mary had a strong *moral* "sex education" in the home in which she was raised. Would she have been adequately prepared to be the mother of the Son of God if she had not been so educated? Why?

B. Try to imagine Mary's and Joseph's emotions when Jesus was missing for three days and describe how you think they felt. Was Jesus' whereabouts the fault of the temple leaders or a form of adolescent rebellion? Is adolescent rebellion a sin? Define "sin." Do you think Jesus' parents would have been justified in punishing Him since He was not held from them against His will? Is there a difference between sinlessness and behavioral perfection? (Consider Exodus 20:12.)

C. Jesus appears to have been rude to Mary just before He performed His first miracle or "sign." Do you agree that Mary might have confronted Jesus with the reality of His own call to His ministry? Why?

D. Try to describe the agony of this mother witnessing the execution of her Son for crimes He did not commit. Mary is regarded as the "Queen of Mothers." What does her life tell us about the role of a mother?

E. How would Mary have responded to Jesus' resurrection and the event of Pentecost, both of which she witnessed?

Chapter 3—Herod: A Tyrannical Genius

A. History is replete with the names of brilliant, aggressive geniuses who "sold out" to evil. Can you name a few from history and from our present time?

B. What are some of the common personality traits which are evident in all of them?

C. How have they all tried to use religion as a tool to gain power?

D. Does this nullify the value of religion as a system of corporate morality and worship?

E. What is the difference between "religion" and "personal faith"?

F. Do we need both "religion" and "personal faith" in an organized, civilized society?

G. What happens when one or the other breaks down?

Chapter 4— John the Baptist: A Rugged Individualist

A. Considering the type of home he came from, why do you think John the Baptist took the Nazarite vows?

B. Judging by the Baptizer's reaction to seeing Jesus come to him at the Jordan River, do you think he had any concept of being the forerunner of the Son of God before then? How might he have seen the meaning of his own ministry before then?

C. Many Bible scholars believe that Jesus did not fully understand His mission in life until after the voice of God spoke at His baptism, the dove came upon Him, and John revealed His purpose. Do you agree? Why?

D. Many religionists, along with King Herod Antipas, feared the Baptizer. Was it because of the crowds he drew or because of the power of his message? What were some characteristics of both the crowds and his message?

E. Should the Christian ministry generate similar reactions today as described in Question D? Would these reactions result in some suffering similar to that of John the Baptist's? Is this happening in our time? Can you recite examples?

F. Of all people, John the Baptist's doubts about Jesus' authenticity seem strange. He was second only to Thomas in this. Notice in both cases how Jesus responded to an honest doubter. Explain the statement, "A doubt is a door."

Chapter 5—Nicodemus: A Puzzled Clergyman

A. Was Nicodemus' fears of his peers justified?

B. Try to put yourself in a "frame of mind" similar to Nicodemus when he first came to Jesus at night. How would you react if Jesus abruptly told you, "You must be born again?"

C. Nicodemus became known in history as a "secret disciple" of Jesus. How would God regard such a person in judgement?

D. In John 3:5, during this most famous interview of all time, Jesus spoke of being born of water and the Spirit. Does "water" refer to the process of physical birth or baptism? Does baptism save us? Does the Spirit of God save us?

E. If Nicodemus happened to remember what Jesus had told him in John 3:14, what "thunderbolt" thought would have struck him when he found himself up on the cross in the process of helping Joseph of Arimathea (another "secret disciple") remove the body of Jesus for burial?

F. Memorize John 3:16 and 17, the key verses to the New Testament. Can you describe the meaning of the word "so" in verse 16?

Chapter 6—A Woman Caught in the Act

A. The law of the land declares that a person shall have only one spouse at a time. Does this satisfy the law of God? Why?

B. In many societies, sexual intercourse between consenting adults outside the marriage bond is not judged under statutory law as a punishable crime except in the case of prostitution. Does this satisfy the law of God? Why?

C. Would public humiliation be an effective way to prevent crime or immorality? Or would it be regarded as a cruel and unusual punishment?

D. Who would be more likely to be held responsible for an immoral act—the man or the woman?

E. Is the plague of AIDS today, even among innocent child victims, a punishment given by God for immorality in our society?

F. Compare the concept of humiliation and punishment with the way Jesus regarded this woman. Which would be more effective in prevention of moral crimes in the future?

Chapter 7— John: A Spoiled Brat

A. Given the kind of persons that John and his brother James were as young men, why do you suppose Jesus ever chose them to be His disciples?

B. Probably more people are won to Jesus Christ through reading or hearing the words of the Gospel of John than any other portion of the Bible. What characteristics of John's background and personality would indicate that he had an understanding of the deep meaning of conversion to Christ that was far above average?

C. Why could it be said that the "disciple whom Jesus loved," as John refers to himself in his Gospel, was so described because Jesus was the *only* Person who genuinely loved him, not that Jesus loved him more than the other disciples?

D. Once John's life had been "turned around" by Christ, his commitment was sustained

for the rest of his very long life. He became
known as "the *Beloved* Apostle." Later in
John's life, there were some who taught
that Jesus was not truly human, but only a
divine ghost. Why then would John so strong-
ly defend the idea of Jesus Christ being the
only Son of God in human form, as in his
Gospel and his letters? (For example, see
First John 1:1 and Second John 10–11.)

E. Do you agree with this doctrine: "With God
there is no love without justice, nor is there
justice without love?" Explain this.

Chapter 8— Martha, Mary and Lazarus: A Close-
Knit Family

A. Do you blame Martha for being upset with
Mary for not helping her prepare dinner for
Jesus and His disciples? Why?

B. Taking the text of Jesus' response to Mar-
tha literally, do you think Jesus made
Martha feel better toward either Mary or
Himself?

C. If you had been in Jesus' shoes, would you
have responded to Martha's complaint dif-
ferently? How?

D. If there is a "spat" between family members
or between friends, does it necessarily have
to reduce their love for each other? What

does holding a "grudge" do to friends or a family? What does it do to the "grudge bearer"?

E. It appears that this very human Jesus did not plan on raising Lazarus from the dead until He actually arrived at his grave. Why? Could it be that the Divine Christ was moved to do His greatest miracle or "sign" (before His own resurrection) through the words that He spoke to Martha, and then to Mary?

F. Examining closely the Gospel of John, Chapter 11, how did Jesus Christ prove Himself to be One with God the Creator?

G. Since John is the only Gospel writer who reported the raising of Lazarus from the dead, are you able to believe this report? Explain your conclusion.

End of Real Discoveries for Volume I

You are encouraged to continue
these studies in Volume II.

Bibliography

Augsburger, Myron S. *Matthew*. The Communicator's Commentary Series, Gen. Ed. Lloyd John Ogilivie, vol. 1. Waco, Texas: Word Books, Inc., 1982.

Cedar, Paul A. *James, First and Second Peter.* The Communicator's Commentary Series, Gen. Ed. Lloyd John Ogilivie, vol. 11. Waco, Texas: Word Books, Inc., 1982.

Cruden, Alexander. *Cruden's Complete Concordance.* Philadelphia: The John C. Winston Publishing Company, 1930.

Fredrickson, Roger L. *John.* The Communicator's Commentary Series, Gen. Ed. Lloyd John Ogilivie, vol. 4. Waco, Texas: Word Books, Inc., 1982.

The International Standard Bible Encyclopedia. Gen. Ed., James Orr. vols. 1-5. Chicago: Howard-Severance Company, 1915.

Larson, Bruce. *Luke.* The Communicator's Commentary Series, Gen. Ed. Lloyd John Ogilivie, vol. 3. Waco, Texas: Word Books, Inc., 1982.

McKenna, David L. *Mark.* The Communicator's Commentary Series, Gen. Ed. Lloyd John Ogilivie, vol. 2. Waco, Texas: Word Books, Inc., 1982.

Nave, Orville J. *Nave's Topical Bible.* Lincoln, Nebraska: Topical Bible Publishing Company, 1905.

The New Testament, King James Version (with Pictures). New York: American Bible Society, 1963.

Ogilivie, Lloyd John. *Acts.* The Communicator's Commentary Series, Gen. Ed. Lloyd John Ogilivie, vol. 5. Waco, Texas: Word Books, Inc., 1982.

Palmer, Earl F. *First, Second, Third John and Revelation.* The Communicator's Commentary Series, Gen. Ed. Lloyd John Ogilivie, vol. 12. Waco, Texas: Word Books, Inc., 1982.

The Works of Josephus: New Updated Edition, Complete and Unabridged. Compiler, M.S. Peabody. Translator, William Whiston. Peabody, Massachusetts: Hendrickson Publishers, 1987.

All Biblical quotations taken from *The Holy Bible, New International Version*, International Bible Society: Colorado Springs, Colorado, 1984.

GIVE A GIFT WHICH WILL PROVIDE A LIFETIME OF ENCOURAGEMENT AND SPIRITUAL STRENGTH!

Written in uncomplicated and everyday language, but with thought-provoking depth, even one who is only a casual reader will not easily lay it aside. Share what you have found in *JESUS CHRIST AT FACE VALUE; Is He for Real?, Volume 1,* with those who are just getting acquainted with who Jesus is. The contents and thought-provoking questions found in this book will be ideal to use with your Bible study group of high school age or older. It will stimulate a lively response and curiosity. You will find it hard to close a discussion on each chapter.

Additional copies of *JESUS CHRIST AT FACE VALUE: Is He for Real?, Volume 1,* may be obtained directly from the Author for $8.00 each, which includes tax, shipping and handling. Please allow 4 to 6 weeks for delivery.

JESUS CHRIST AT FACE VALUE; Is He for Real?, Volume II, will soon be available at $7.00 per copy. It will bring to you new insights about Simon Peter, Pontius Pilate, Judas Iscariot, Simon of Cyrene, Mary Magdalene, a woman near death, and Thomas—in a similar style as Volume I. These personalities were quite different than you may have been told in the past! RESERVE YOUR COPY NOW!

Rev. James L. Unger, Sr., the author, is available for book presentations and speaking engagements. Also, please let us know what you think of Jesus Christ after reading this book.

Send all correspondence to the address on the Order Form.

Order From:
Rev. James L. Unger, Sr.,
P.O. Box 40472
Bakersfield, CA 93384-0472

For each copy of *Jesus Christ at Face Value; Is He for Real?, Volume I,* please send $8.00 in check or money order (no cash or stamps) and this form with the information completed. Price includes tax, shipping, and handling. Please allow 4–6 weeks for delivery.

Send me _____ copies of *Jesus Christ at Face Value; Is He for Real?, Volume I* at $8.00 each.

Total Enclosed $ _____

NAME _____

ADDRESS_____ APT. NO. _____

CITY _____ STATE _____ ZIP _____

PHONE (Optional) _____

☐ Please reserve for me _____ copies of *Jesus Christ at Face Value; Is He for Real? Volume II.* When available, please send details.

THE BATTLE FOR THE SEED by Dr. Patricia Morgan. The dilemma facing young people today is a major concern for all parents. Teen suicide is at an all-time high. Unwanted pregnancies make the womb one of the most dangerous places on earth. These conditions did not happen over-night, nor will ignoring them cause the scenario to suddenly disappear. This important book of the 90's shows God's way to change the condition of the young and advance God's purpose for every nation into the next century. TPB-112p. ISBN 1-56043-099-0 Retail $7.95